*The title says it all.....what a great book! An easy, enjoyable and entertaining read. Laurence Seton presents a simple but highly effective project management system that in my 28 year career is among one of the easiest, most effective I have come across.*

**Brian Milloy, Director Business Development, Sierra Systems Group Inc.**

*The Projecteze system is awesome! The book "On Top Of Everything" had me up and running with it in only three days. Almost immediately, I went from flipping back through pages in my project notebook and facing hundreds of active emails to having everything together in my Projecteze Table ........ and an empty inbox. Instead of second guessing myself and wondering what I might have forgotten, now I spend my time proactively directing my projects and staying on top of everything.*

**Al Massicotte, Lead-Pipeline Projects West, Canadian Natural Resources Ltd**

*Now that I've been exposed to Projecteze I can't imagine performing my job without it. I don't leave the office with the stress of wondering what has to be done at work the next day. I just come in, open up my Projecteze Table and start working.*

**Brian Celaire, Project Engineer, Cenovus Energy Inc.**

*Your ability to plan and complete projects is essential to your income, success and productivity, and Projecteze shows you exactly how to do it.*

**Brian Tracy, Best Selling Author & Professional Speaker**

*When I was introduced to the Projecteze system, I was amazed at how simple but powerful it is. It allows one to control and filter all the demands and requests that are placed on us daily.*

**Tom Fransham, VP Engineering & Design, IMV Projects Inc.**

*Projecteze has revolutionized my life! Every day I am grateful for my Projecteze Table. Thank you so much for a simply wonderful system.*

**Kristie Demke, President, Professional Organizers in Canada**

*Laurence has written a phenomenal book. The explicit examples from so many different areas of life (work, home, school, vacations) are enhanced by real life stories. This book is a gold mine! People who want to get and stay organized will love it!*
Sheila Artus, Manager PM Office, Shaw Communications Inc.

*The Projecteze system is so simple that it borders on brilliance.*
George Roberts, George Roberts & Co.

*Projecteze is without a doubt one of the best project management tools I have ever come across. This is definitely a book that has inspired me to take my project management skills to a whole new level. I recommend this book for newbies as well as seasoned professionals who are looking to find a way to get more time out of their days.*
Derek Major, Founder & CEO, Eligeo IT

*The power of Projecteze lies in its simplicity and flexibility! Using software I already have, I no longer feel overwhelmed and I'm accomplishing what is most important each day. For the first time ever I feel "on top of everything" both professionally and personally. The applications are endless!*
Laura Watson, President, Venture Coaching Inc.

*Anyone who has made the decision to get control of their commitments and who has the will power to systematize their time management process can surely gain from adopting and customizing Projecteze to their needs. I can also see how the productivity of a team of people could be improved by use of this tool.*
Dr Janice Thomas, Program Director, MBA in Project Management,
Athabasca University

*I have been using this simple yet powerfully effective tool for a month now and the positive benefits have manifested themselves in so many ways! First and foremost, Projecteze provides me with a clear plan of action for my daily work activities. As a result, Projecteze has reduced my work stress which is improving my overall personal health and wellness.*
Allison Zukewich, Quality Advisor, Total E&P Canada Ltd

*I have been using Projecteze for a few weeks now and wow, what a difference it has made in my world! I had previously tried using several different systems ranging from a To-Do list on a piece of paper, to a specific industry based solution to Outlook and found that none of them really gave me an overview of what was truly on my plate. Projecteze is easy to use, it helps me stay on top of all my work and I find myself breathing more easily because of it.*

Jennifer Chipperfield, Chipperfield Photography

# On Top Of Everything™

## Manage Your Projects & Life With Ease

Projecteze®: The Ultimate Organizational System

Laurence H. Seton, P.Eng., PMP

On Top Of Everything™
Manage Your Projects & Life With Ease
Projecteze®: The Ultimate Organizational System
By Laurence H. Seton, P.Eng., PMP

**Published by:** Projecteze Inc., Calgary, Alberta, Canada
**Website:** www.OnTopOfEverything.com
**Editor:** Carol Sheehan, CS Communication Strategies, Comox, British Columbia
**Cover/Book Design:** Nelson Vigneault, Calgary, Alberta, Canada

First Edition, Third Printing (2012)
Edition ISBNs
Soft Cover        978-0-9810629-0-7
PDF               978-0-9810629-1-4

Library and Archives Canada Cataloguing in Publication
Seton, Laurence, 1953-
On top of everything: manage your projects & life with ease: Projecteze,
the ultimate organizational system / Laurence Seton.
Includes bibliographical references.
ISBN 978-0-9810629-0-7
1. Project management. 2. Industrial productivity. 3. Organization. I. Title.
HD69.P75S48 2009   658.4'04   C2008-904544-0

**Printed in Canada**

# Contents

## Introduction

*An innovation, to be effective,*
*has to be simple and it has to be focused.*
–Peter Drucker

### Is This System For You?

I wrote this book for busy people who deal with complex and diverse projects and whose goals are to stay organized, be on top of everything, and live a balanced life with time for themselves. They already use computers, tablets and smart phones.

They include:
Consultants
Entrepreneurs
Professionals
Managers
Project Managers
Executives
Administrators
Executive Assistants
Students and Teachers

Many of these people use productivity tools to help them deal with high volumes of information, an increasing workload, and greater demands on their time. They have a sense that the systems they currently use are either inadequate for handling the diverse range of responsibilities they manage or are too cumbersome or complex to maintain. They often feel stressed out and overwhelmed.

How many emails do you receive in a day–10, 20, 50, 100, 200? It's not unusual for many of us to receive 50 to 100 emails in a day on top of all the meetings we have to attend, reports we have to write and projects we have to manage. And then we go home to more emails, voice mails, kids with homework and sports, and an endless list of personal responsibilities.

We are dealing with overloaded schedules, escalating demands and increasing complexity. And many of us are just barely managing to keep up because our days are so full.

**Do you recognize yourself in any of these statements?**

- You wish you had more time for yourself.
- You wish you had more quality time for your loved ones.
- You feel overwhelmed and burned out.
- You are always stressed from continually having to put out fires.
- Your head is filled with clutter from everything you have to remember.
- You have a difficult time relaxing and letting go.
- Your relationships at work and at home are not what they could be.

This book is about providing busy people with an effective system that will help them stay on top of everything in their lives and be more available for what is most important.

**In order to benefit from this system:**

- You will use a computer regularly.
- You will use a readily available software application.
- You will commit to using the system consistently.

The biggest challenge people face is not with using the Projecteze system, but in using the system *consistently*. The system itself is easy to master. You will however, need to make a concerted effort to use the system methodically–daily–for at least one month to realize its full value. Give it a month and you should expect see an improvement in your performance and how you feel about your work, and your life. From there it just keeps getting better.

Laurence Seton © | Projecteze Inc.

## A Solemn Vow and the Origins of This System

*I'm going to be like you Dad,*
*you know I'm going to be like you.*
—Harry Chapin, lyric from *Cats In The Cradle*

As early as I can remember, I cherished the company of my father. He was a great guy and a hero to me. And he was a hero in the truest sense of the word. As a World War II fighter-bomber pilot, he was awarded the Distinguished Flying Cross. After the war, Dad returned to North America, went back to school and started a long and successful career as an architect. As a child, I adored him and wanted to be just like him.

Starting early in his career he put in extra hours at home. He would place me in my crib on the other side of the large room where he was working at his drafting table. I learned how to get the crib to move across the floor by throwing what little weight I had into one end of it. It took me ages to get over to him, but I did—repeatedly. My reward was to be allowed to sit on his lap for a while. A few years later, I remember Dad coaching me on how to memorize the names of my model cars. Any time I could spend with him was special, and I eagerly absorbed his teachings and his presence.

As I grew older, Dad became more and more immersed in his career, and I became more aware of a consistent pattern in our lives. My father was less and less available for those cherished times together. After a long day at the office, he would come home and we'd have dinner together as a family; then shortly after, Dad would disappear into his home office to work. And we wouldn't see him for the rest of the evening. This quickly became the norm.

As I moved into my teens, I vowed that I would never allow myself to become so consumed by my job that I would detach from my family. This philosophy worked well until I started my own career and became a parent myself. All of a sudden, my vow wasn't so easy to keep. As I chose the roles of employee, husband and father, life became busier and busier. And adhering to my principle of not being swallowed up by my work became more difficult. My life grew more and more complex and crowded.

As a professional engineer and project manager, I moved into a high-speed world filled with important details and overlapping complexities. I often found they would keep me awake at night, project details repeating over and over again in my head. My mind raced while I tried to sleep, the details filling every moment.

At work, I remember feeling so overwhelmed and stressed that I would develop headaches. The relentless pace and escalating sense of urgency left me feeling both mentally and physically exhausted. I felt completely disconnected from any sense of peace, and I knew from experience that the relationships that mattered the most to me were suffering. Before long, I could see I was living a life that was not unlike my father's. I knew I had to break the pattern. Surely it was possible to stay in my chosen profession without having to endure the perpetual stress and feelings of being overwhelmed that characterized my then normal state of being.

Knowing I was ultimately responsible for my own situation, I could see that the solution laid in the way I responded to things and the way I organized my life. I knew I needed to live my life differently. Convinced that there must be a better alternative—I started to appreciate the difference between *having a full life* and *living a fulfilling life*. I became very motivated to change.

## Searching For A Solution

Early on, as I searched for a solution, I learned an important lesson: when I was well organized, I was able to be more pro-active, I could relax more easily and I enjoyed more personal freedom. I found that being organized created space and "freed up time" which took a bit of the pressure off. Periodically, I could pull my head out of the details, enjoy life, and more fully appreciate the people and things around me. When I was well organized, life didn't always seem like a mad rush. The problem was, despite my efforts, I could never stay fully organized.

In my pursuit of finding the perfect organizational solution, I used many different personal productivity tools to improve my effectiveness. I used paper-based systems such as Day-Timer® and TimeText® to some benefit. Computers brought about new possibilities, but many computer-based and hand-held systems, despite all their promises, were rigid in their structure and lacked the flexibility to deal with diverse and complex information from within their standard tool kits.

Throughout my career, I have used more robust and complicated project management tools. I tried to adapt these to meet my organizational needs, but I realized very quickly that fully fledged project management systems were overly complex for my purposes. They lacked the ability to simply and easily help me manage my team and myself during a project, especially when I was working on several different projects at a time, for many different clients.

Finding a workable solution turned out to be a bigger challenge than I had anticipated. After years of frustrating trial and error with personal productivity and project management tools, I decided to develop my own solution.

## Developing the Ultimate Solution

*In order to go from brilliance to wisdom,*
*you have to pass through simple.*
−Marilyn Ferguson

I wanted to be "on top of everything" but not just for the sake of being hyper-organized. Being hyper-organized was worthless if I became more efficient at the cost of my relationships and especially my home life. I wanted to carve out some space for myself−for family and personal time. I wanted to succeed at my career without being swallowed up by it. I wanted to be available for what was most important in my life.

It occurred to me that I needed a third option, "a hybrid tool", a blended productivity and project management tool that was simple yet sophisticated enough to help me manage myself within a multi-client, multi-project environment. It had to help me see the forest *and* the trees.

Despite a relentless search, I could not find a system that provided the mix of features I was looking for. I needed a practical system that was:

1) Simple−so it wouldn't be a chore to set up and use.

2) Flexible−to deal with roles and accountabilities across many projects and many clients.

3) Adaptable−to store relevant information, no matter how detailed, for how ever many projects I threw at it.

So, I ended up creating my own highly effective solution−
a method I call *Projecteze®: The Ultimate Organizational System.*

## Ten Years Later

Fast-forward ten years. Now I can't imagine working the way I used to. As a professional engineer and project manager, I have worked on many projects with significant budgets in a variety of environments. Using the Projecteze system, I have been able to deal with more diversity and complexity than I would have thought possible when I began my career. What is equally rewarding is that I have a rich and fulfilling life with wonderful relationships both at work and at home. I am an active parent and I have time for hobbies, sports and personal pursuits. With Projecteze, I realized the objective I set for myself as a teenager.

My secret weapons have been the Projecteze system, my own diligence in using it to stay on top of everything, and my choice to be more available for life.

This book will share the actual mechanics of the Projecteze system—which won't take long to learn because the system is incredibly simple. The rest of the book focuses on helping you understand how to apply the system and customize it to suit your own needs.

My goal is to help you achieve the success you want without sacrificing your life in the process. I want to help you regain control of your life.

# I

## Projecteze:
## The Ultimate Organizational System

*Furious activity does not necessarily equate to progress
and is no substitute for understanding.*
—Anonymous

## The Evolution of Information Overload

Not so many generations ago, life was simpler. It used to be that a person's workload might have amounted to a handful of things to accomplish in a day. The daily pace was much slower then, and there were only a few core tasks to focus on, usually one at a time—feeding the chickens, milking the cows, plowing the fields, and watching the sun go down. Compared to today, there was a lot less that required our urgent attention.

It is hard to believe how much life has changed just since the invention of the computer. The first personal computers came out in the late 1970s and early 1980s and the nature of work became more complex. With this new technology, people were not only able to save their work in progress, but they could manipulate ideas and data more easily and with greater efficiency than ever before. This was a revolutionary change that altered expectations of how fast we could respond to requests and what we could accomplish in a day.

The fax machine became commercially available and widely used only as recently as the late 1980s. Written and visual communication could be shared with anyone around the world in minutes. With this enhanced connectivity, our lives sped up another notch and the time frame for exchanging information advanced from days to mere hours. Since then, email has compressed interaction times to minutes—even seconds. Today, instant text messaging says it all. Talk about life speeding up!

The evolution of information technology brought with it the expectation of immediate interaction with and response from other people. This phenomenon resulted in greater productivity, but the pace of the average workday also increased and became more stressful. Information overload became the norm rather than the exception as expectations accelerated with every new advance in data processing and communications. Comparatively, we can only look back enviously at past generations and their relationship with time.

   Laurence Seton © | Projecteze Inc.

Life may have improved in many ways, but now one of our key challenges is to figure out how to cope with the relentless barrage of information and a steady increase in the complexity of daily life. Today we typically have hundreds of items to process in a day. We feel a continual pressure to coordinate with dozens of people, prioritize, delegate, keep our focus on several often-conflicting objectives—and still see the big picture. Most of us have simply become busier and busier, and as a result, we sacrifice precious time that could be devoted to our relationships and to ourselves. Many find it more and more difficult to maintain any sense of balance.

Without balance, all of this "busy-ness" can lead to elevated stress levels. Working harder, longer and smarter as a means to cope only works for a while. As soon as we learn how to handle one level of overload and free up some space in our calendar, we just fill it with more work as we strive to somehow handle an even greater degree of complexity and volume.

This spiral of more and faster leads to either hyper-efficiency or burnout. More than likely, at some point our support systems break down and we get stressed out, burned out—or worse. What can we do to take charge of this ever-accelerating cycle?

**What Do the Best of the Best Do?**

*All project managers face problems on Monday mornings—*
*good project managers are working on next Monday's problems.*
—Anonymous

In any profession, there are always a few who excel beyond the norm. This is true in project management as well. So, what separates the best project managers from the rest? In his book *Alpha Project Managers: What the Top 2% Know That Everyone Else Does Not*, Andy Crowe describes his findings from an extensive survey of project managers. Based on meeting certain criteria, including scores on key performance indicators, the top 2% who excelled above others in their profession were designated as "Alpha Project Managers".

Crowe's key findings include:

1) Nearly all of the Alphas demonstrated two key abilities associated with having a system to help them prioritize work and maintain focus on a project's critical success factors.

- The first was the ability to sift through massive amounts of information, extract only the most important components, and sort the information appropriately. (2006:70)

- The second was "the ability to establish and maintain priorities on both a higher, strategic level and a lower, tactical level." (2006:70) A vast majority of the Alpha group were dedicated to the discipline of regularly reviewing their priorities.

2) A universal theme among the Alphas is that they have solid relational skills. "Many revealed in post-survey interviews that their success at managing projects was proportional to the strength of their relationships." (2006:185)

A key point to take from Crowe's work is the importance of having the discipline to use a system on a regular basis to set and maintain priorities, handle information overload, plan ahead, support relationship building, and maintain a sense of balance.

### Existing Productivity Systems and Unworkable Gaps

*My mechanic told me, "I couldn't repair your brakes,*
*so I made your horn louder."*
—Steven Wright

Over the past 30 years, I have used many personal productivity and project management systems and tools. Each one carried some merit, but I never found a system that provided me with everything I was looking for. There was always something missing, an unworkable gap to contend with.

There were the hand-written systems such as Day-Timer™ and Time Text™. Many of these paper-based systems featured variations on a consistent theme: managing a workload from a list of daily *To Dos*. Each day I would complete what I could and any remaining items had to be hand-written onto the next day's page. If these were low-priority tasks, this process could go on for days or even weeks. I got sick and tired of re-writing these tasks, continually having to bring them forward and, as I did this each day, having them remind me of where I had failed to complete an objective. This process frequently left me feeling that I'd dropped the ball, even though these tasks had to be left undone in order to attend to much higher priorities. If I wanted to stop carrying those lower priority tasks forward, it meant I would have to transfer them to some other list or lose them altogether.

Then there were systems that advocated maintaining separate lists—perhaps one for each project or objective. This complicated matters and multiplied the time required to stay organized across a group of projects.

Other systems proposed using a physical bring-forward file where you had to transfer items from one physical file to another physical file. This resulted in increased paper filing and moved me away from the ideal efficiency of handling documents only once.

PDAs and smart phones upgraded the *To Do List* concept by making it digital. Using these systems, I no longer needed to manually bring tasks forward, but these devices tended to be overly simplistic in terms of their ability to group tasks by project and by client. Descriptions had to be kept very brief and the information could only be viewed in limited ways (often only by priority or by date). This approach was insufficient for handling the complexity of what I had to deal with each day. I also found that benefits from electronic *To Do* lists were often offset by an increase in information overload because I had to learn a new device and its accompanying software. Perhaps the most troublesome aspect of these electronic *To Do* lists was the complicated and error-prone process of synchronizing my mobile device with both my work and home computers.

Microsoft Outlook is a great example of a basic task management *To Do List* and calendar system. Outlook offers a fine interface for basic organization and group collaboration, but as soon as I tried to use it for multi-project or multi-client situations, its usefulness plummeted. It simply could not handle the complexity effectively.

We often associate organizing vast amounts of information with spreadsheets; however, for me there were some less than appealing aspects associated with using them for tracking and managing project information. Spreadsheets have limited formatting options and limit the number of characters that can be presented in each cell. If the number of characters is extensive, they will often be truncated on the screen and on the printed copy. This restricts the amount of information that can be effectively used in any one cell.

Microsoft Project and Primavera® are common examples of project scheduling software. They work very well for the comprehensive scheduling of a project. The overwhelming challenge with this kind of software is that these are not simple programs; there is a steep and lengthy learning curve associated with them. They serve their purpose of scheduling and tracking projects very well, but for my purposes, I primarily wanted to focus on how to effectively manage myself and the responsibilities assigned to team members. That is an entirely different focus.

Another organizational alternative was on-line collaboration systems. Collaborative solutions expose one's own performance to the degree of involvement by other team members. If others don't provide accurate or timely input, the effectiveness of the tool as a whole decreases to the point that it won't maintain credibility with the team, and its use progressively diminishes. First and foremost, I needed to be able to manage my own responsibilities for the projects I was working on.

When I realized that none of the individual systems I tried could provide me with what I needed, I tried to combine systems. I thought that maybe if I combined individual systems, I could make the combination work for me. The resulting process was overly complex and unmanageable. It always involved a complicated coordination of separate documents and systems that took too much time and effort to manage.

Over the past three decades there have been numerous time management and project management systems that have come onto the market. You name it, I've tried it. After an exhaustive search, I was never able to find any one system that worked the way I needed it to.

Current personal productivity systems, be they paper-based or computerized (Microsoft Outlook, PDAs and smart phones), failed me on four fronts:

1) They were operationally too complicated to coordinate work between office, mobile, and home—especially when this involved more than one computer platform (i.e. Mac® vs. PC).

2) They were financially expensive, but, even more importantly, they were expensive in terms of the extensive time and work investment required to realize any value from them.

3) They were unsophisticated, inflexible or restrictive in terms of their ability to work with complex project information (client, project, task, priority, delegation and accountability).

4) They were limited in their ability to format and present information in a user-friendly manner.

In general, I found that existing personal productivity and project management systems were either too simplistic, too complex, too demanding or too structurally rigid.

I needed to find a better solution.

## Being Hyper-Efficient and Balanced

*I put instant coffee in a microwave oven*
*and almost went back in time.*
–Steven Wright

There is an inherent challenge built into personal productivity objectives: I can eventually become hyper-efficient if I really work at it. I can always be more efficient. I can always get better at handling large volumes of information and managing the increasing complexity of completing tasks and delegating work. The problem with striving to become hyper-efficient is that it can be a trap. It never ends. There is no point of arrival. The pace, volume, and scope can just go on expanding–more and more, faster and faster until you or your system reach a limit and break down.

Any motivation I have for being increasingly efficient must include some aspect of personal purpose. It needs to include a personal goal such as: "I will be hyper-efficient in order to have more quality time for my family and myself." This is a very real and tangible reward that motivates me. In fact, it describes the lifestyle balance I have strived for since my teenage years.

Working in an accelerating environment for more than 30 years, I have witnessed and experienced first-hand the stress associated with the escalating cycle of more efficiency, which begets more responsibility, which in turn demands more efficiency, which then begets even more responsibility–etcetera, etcetera.

Dealing with the need for hyper-efficiency presents two core challenges:

1) What will enable me to effectively handle an escalating volume and complexity of information?

2) What will help me avoid the trap of simply filling space I create with more work?

Laurence Seton © | Projecteze Inc.

## Creating Space

*The human brain can only hold about seven pieces*
*of information for less than 30 seconds!...*
*If you want to extend the 30 seconds to a few minutes or*
*even an hour or two, you will need to consistently re-expose*
*yourself to the information.*
—John Medina

How do we balance the equation?

Hundreds of authors have written articles and books on how to improve personal effectiveness. A common theme has been the need to create space in our lives so that occasionally we can step back to see the big picture, and in turn, make better choices about what is important versus what is simply urgent. Our relationships very often depend on this.

In his book, *First Things First*, Stephen Covey describes how we tend to get pulled into work that is "urgent and important," dousing fires that need to be put out immediately, and in the process all too often letting others set our own priorities. This all happens at the expense of not being able to get at work that is "important, but *not* urgent" which includes planning, preparation, prevention, and extremely important relationship activities such as team building, networking and just taking the time to give our complete attention to another person in conversation. The urgent tasks crowd out the equally important non-urgent tasks, forcing us to catch-up during extra hours. (1994:37-41)

In *Getting Things Done*, author David Allen advocates having some mechanism for downloading everything that is on your mind so you can be freer to react more fully to the moment. He recognizes the advantages of downloading mental clutter and freeing yourself for more important big-picture work. Beyond downloading the mental clutter, Allen also observes:

*The ability to be successful, relaxed, and in control during these fertile but turbulent times demands new ways of thinking and working.*

*...There has been a missing piece in our new culture of knowledge work: a system with a coherent set of behaviors and tools that functions effectively at the level at which work really happens. It must incorporate the results of big-picture thinking as well as the smallest of open details. It must manage multiple tiers of priorities. It must maintain control over hundreds of new daily inputs.*

*You need a good system that can keep track of as many of (the things you have to think about and deal with in one day) as possible, supply required information about them on demand, and allow your focus to shift from one thing to the next quickly and easily. (2001:7, 9, 21)*

Covey and Allen both describe why we need a system that can help us download our mental clutter and step back from the urgent issues in our life so we can create space with which to take on the important non-urgent work associated with seeing the big picture and strengthening our relationships.

## My Personal Organizational System

I didn't want a system that would help me become hyper-efficient for the sake of being hyper-efficient. Instead I wanted something that would help me strike a better balance between being efficient and being available for life. I reasoned that with a balance that included being more personally available, I would be able to see the big picture more clearly—and that would help me make better choices in *all* areas of my life.

My goal was to find an organizational system that would help me clear the mental clutter that infringed on my work and home life. It would be able to handle overwhelming volumes of complex information and the dimensions of client, project, task, priority, accountability and delegation. This system would help me stay on top of commitments, both my own and other people's commitments to me. A primary driver for using such a system would be to create space for my work, my relationships, and myself.

Laurence Seton © | Projecteze Inc.

## Requirements For The Ultimate Organizational System

In order to realize the objectives I had identified, my ultimate organizational system would have to satisfy severals specific requirements. A workable solution would have to:

- Help me step back from all the urgencies and demands coming at me.

- Be simple to learn and easy to use.

- Make me aware of my highest priorities and what I should be paying attention to.

- Keep track of everything from one central location.

- Provide me with the relevant information I needed, when I needed it.

- Be flexible and scalable (for multiple projects and multiple clients).

- Help me stay on top of my own commitments and responsibilities, and the commitments others made to me.

- Make it easy to enter and manipulate information (group, sort and prioritize).

- Provide me with both the details and the big picture.

- Be computer-based.

- Have no requirement to buy and learn a new gadget or software.

- Have a low cost – financially and in the time required to learn and use it.

- Be a cross-platform solution – compatible with PC, Mac®, mobile and on-line.

## Constructing My Own System

*To every rule there is an exception,*
*and vice versa.*
—Anonymous

I was frustrated with my inability to make existing systems work so I started experimenting with other ways to manage my information. I wanted a process for knowing exactly what I was accountable for at any time with ready access to the information I needed in order to fulfill those responsibilities. It all boiled down to getting the key information I needed, quickly and easily, when I needed it.

On a whim, I started using tables in Microsoft Word (MS Word) to help me summarize what I wanted from a system. I was already reasonably familiar with MS Word, as are many people, and thought it would be a good tool for capturing what I was looking for. After some trials and adjustments, I came to realize that MS Word has the ability to create surprisingly robust and elegant table structures.

I quickly learned that within an MS Word table I could sort information by any column and that I could embed tables within tables. I was also able to enter a wide variety of information into any cell with full edit, layout and formatting capabilities. The flexibility of cell structure in MS Word tables allowed me to simplify its basic table structure to the point where four columns was all I needed to handle anything a project could throw at me. Suddenly, I realized I had the computerized engine I needed, in a very simple structure.

At first, the idea of using a word processing application to stay organized seemed counter-intuitive. Expecting my die-hard computer-literate colleagues to scoff at the prospect, I was at first reluctant to share this approach with them, but eventually I did. After they saw what I could accomplish with this simple system, they started asking if I would teach them how to use it. Watching them and seeing how easily they adopted the system and realize its benefits, I knew I was on to something.

I continued to test my new system and compare it to what spreadsheets and other existing organizational systems like MS Outlook offered. Nothing else matched the flexibility and range of functionality that tables in MS Word could provide.

I also discovered that most of MS Word's Table features were similar to table functions found in other contemporary word processing tools. Anyone who used a comparably equipped word processor could follow this approach.

Comparing the list of requirements I set for the ultimate organizational system, I found that tables in MS Word provided them all. The reasons for using MS Word's Table function as an organizational tool far out-weighed any arguments against it. It turned out to be an exceptionally elegant solution that provided everything I was looking for.

MS Word was easy to work with, and I already had the software. Its advanced table structure was supplemented by a tremendous flexibility for entering and presenting information. It was compatible with Mac® and PC computer platforms so I could use it equally well at work and at home. It provided a nice balance between being too simplistic and being overly complex. It worked really well.

MS Word's Table function allowed me to:

- Sort by columns within a table, in much the same way I could do with a spreadsheet.

- Be completely flexible with regard to how much information I could enter into any cell.

- Handle both simple and complex data in a way that suited me best, on a case-by-case basis.

- Present data in a sophisticated and friendly manner because of its extensive formatting and highlighting options, making it easy to use and read.

- Use my existing knowledge and experience–there was next to no learning curve, and I already had the software.

- Use the same system to organize my work projects and my home projects.

I decided to call my system *Projecteze®*–a name symbolic of what this system is and what it does. I spent the next ten years working with and refining Projecteze while I took it through its paces, using it to manage a wide variety of projects in three completely different industries. I also used it to track my home maintenance and other personal projects. Projecteze continually held up to everything I threw at it. It never let me down.

Projecteze helped me get and stay "on top of everything" both at work and at home. I became highly productive. I was consistently coming from a place of balance. My relationships were getting the quality time they deserved. I was living the life I had always wanted and promised myself so many years ago.

**Projecteze®: The Ultimate Organizational System**

Projecteze is a simple but elegant organizational system that uses tables in MS Word to capture only the essential information and level of detail *you* need to always be one step ahead on all your projects. A Projecteze Table is a single, centralized location to hold the key commitments and action items for all your projects–from emails, meetings, minutes, telephone conversations, face-to-face conversations, and the myriad of other interactions in your daily life.

Projecteze helps you focus on what *you* need to be paying attention to. The success of the system is based on the premise that if you are always aware of and completing your most important and highest priority tasks, this will naturally lead to a successful outcome on your projects. Projecteze focuses only on what still needs to be done and does not track what has already been completed, which is the job of more sophisticated project management software.

# A Sample Projecteze Table

The following is a sample Projecteze Table. Notice that it only has four columns: Project, Date (next action date for each row), Priority (for the next action item in the row), and Commitments & Action Items. This sample shows a scenario of an entrepreneur starting up a new business. This table was current for the morning of Sept 22:

| Project | Date | Prty | Commitments & Action Items |
|---|---|---|---|
| Marketing & Advertising | Sept 22 | 1 | • Sept 22: Contact Marketing Consultant for status update on promotional materials; due Sept 25 (Sept 5 meeting)<br>• Oct 1: Draft of Marketing Plan to be finalized (Sept 15 mtg)<br>• Oct 3: Promotional materials must be to printer by Oct 5<br>• Oct 10: Promotional materials due back from printer<br>• Oct 15: Kick off general advertising campaign |
| Website | Sept 22 | 3 | • Do a keyword search to determine most effective terms<br>• Website to be updated based on keyword search |
| Corporate & Legal | Sept 23 | 1 | • Sept 23: Finalize corporate structure with lawyer<br>• Sept 24: Lawyer to submit incorporation<br>• Sept 30 (approx): Receive confirmation of incorporation |
| Banking | Sept 23 | 1 | • Sept 23: Call Bank Mgr re: loan application (submitted Sept 15)<br>• Sept 24: Initiate credit card merchant application |
| Accounting | Sept 25 | 2 | • Sept 25: Accountant to have proposal to me for signing (Sept 10 mtg)<br>• Sept 25: Load new accounting software package<br>• Sept 27: Read software manual on the weekend |
| Government | Sept 29 | 2 | • Apply for government taxation accounts |
| Facility | Oct 1 | 1 | • Oct 1: Contact broker about finding office space - for move in by Dec 20; 2,500 sq ft & 3 yr lease preferred |
| Product Line | Oct 2 | 1 | • Oct 2: Set up mtg with associates to review entire product line before Oct 14 |
| Clients | Oct 8 | 1 | • Oct 8: Prepare list of all potential clients with Mgmt Team<br>• Oct 16: Kick-off sales meetings with prospective clients |
| Licensing | Oct 15 | 3 | • Oct 15: Submit business license application<br>• Oct 30: Business license approval should be confirmed |

This sample illustrates many different aspects of a Projecteze Table. It might look overly simplistic, but there is more here than meets the eye. In this example, each row is dedicated to a different aspect of starting up a new business. You can see how easy it is to organize information in the Commitment & Action Items column and that the table is primarily sorted by the Date column. If you are managing many different projects, you can structure your Projecteze Table so that each row is dedicated to a separate project. This structure provides both a detailed list of key priorities for each project as well as the ability to very quickly scan across all your projects. At a glance you gain a perspective on the bigger picture of everything you are working on.

When a person builds a Projecteze Table, it is a personal table for themselves. It contains the commitments and action items that impact them directly and that they need to follow up on, including commitments they have made to others and commitments others have made to them. When you can keep track of and follow up on commitments others have made to you, things get done instead of being forgotten.

## What Makes Projecteze So Effective?

*A pessimist sees the difficulty in every opportunity;*
*an optimist sees the opportunity in every difficulty.*
—Winston Churchill

The Projecteze system is so simple, easy to learn and use that the only challenge remaining is having the discipline to use it. Projecteze requires the same self-discipline that is needed to make good project management a habit. The more you use this system, the more you and your project teams will benefit from it.

Projecteze eliminates any excuses for not using it because it is not restricted by a limitation in technology; using tables in MS Word is simple, easy to learn and easy to apply. Once you embrace the daily practice of using it, you will come to understand just how powerful the disciplined use of Projecteze can be. Properly applied, Projecteze helps you focus on doing what you need to in order to apply yourself most effectively and get your work done.

By applying the necessary discipline to use Projecteze on a consistent and regular (daily) basis, there are many features you will come to appreciate:

1) With Projecteze, you will demonstrate to others you are completely responsible, reliable and accountable for commitments you've made. It will also help you hold others accountable for their commitments in a way that is non-confrontational but very effective.

2) Your Projecteze Table will bring your key commitments and action items into focus when you need to be reminded about them. It makes sure you're aware of your highest priority items at all times.

3) Projecteze lets you respond to new challenges and unexpected surprises with the utmost calmness, efficiency and completeness, knowing your response will be as effective as possible because you will have a comprehensive understanding of the relative priorities of all your commitments and action items. You will find you're much better prepared for dealing with whatever new issues each day throws at you.

4) Your Projecteze Table will change according to how many commitments and action items you have to keep track of—it grows when there is more for you to deal with and then shrinks as items are completed. *It is a living document that is dynamically efficient* because it doesn't simply continue to grow in size as your projects progress.

5) Projecteze is not meant to replace your daily calendar for scheduling meetings but to complement it, so you are well prepared for those meetings and can focus on the most important issues at hand.

6) Projecteze can be used in evey business and industry, it can be applied everywhere from the CEO's office to

the student's desk, and it can be used for anything from managing many concurrent projects to coordinating school work or organizing group events.

7) When you go home at the end of the day, you can leave your work at work because it's all captured, well organized and waiting for you the next day in your Projecteze Table. This system eliminates mental clutter, puts you back in control of your life and helps you find a healthy work-life balance.

8) Projecteze is a system you can use for the rest of your life—from the classroom to the office to home.

**Is Projecteze Meant for You?**

Projecteze is designed for individuals who care about keeping commitments and who are willing to develop a daily practice for staying on top of everything.

Projecteze may not be for everyone. It is *not* for you if:

- You do not like to use systems to help you get and stay organized.

- You do not have access to a computer or have any interest in using one.

- You are unwilling to exert the discipline required to apply the system on a consistent basis.

Laurence Seton © | Projecteze Inc.

## Personal Boundaries

*The best way you can predict your future*
*is to create it.*
–Stephen Covey

The Projecteze system works very well for people who have the discipline to apply it on a consistent basis. As I have described, it can free up time for you to do whatever you choose to do. Unfortunately, we can be drawn to simply fill this time with more work. You can become hyper-efficient and function at a continually escalating level of performance—and in the process, lose a balanced life. This is where personal boundaries come in.

High-energy people may be more active and may choose to take on more because they enjoy the mental stimulation. In short order, they could find themselves trapped into taking on more than they can handle. If you recognize yourself as this kind of person, it may be wise to develop an awareness of when you've crossed the line from enjoying what you're doing to being stressed out by what you've taken on.

To avoid this trap, I recommend you establish healthy boundaries for yourself that reflect how you want to live your life. Ask yourself, "What do I really enjoy doing?" "What do I want to spend my time doing?" Having pre-determined boundaries will help you to know when you've crossed them.

Be proactive about deciding where that freed up time gets spent. Where do you place your family and other relationships in terms of importance in your life? There is a fixed amount of time in a day. Prevent yourself from just becoming busy because you've got some time to fill. Once you come to understand what's important to you, you can choose to live your life in a way that honours those preferences.

Setting personal boundaries is especially important for people in positions that involve fluctuating workloads such as sales, consulting, or management—where people don't have the ability to limit how quickly information and requests are coming at them. By setting boundaries, they can choose to regulate the sense of urgency in their lives and choose how they respond to the barrage of demands for their attention.

With well define personal boundaries, Projecteze can help you live the life you want.

## My Greatest Hope

Using the Projecteze system consistently has enabled me to achieve the lifestyle objectives I set for myself as a teenager. I am able to effectively sift through high volumes of complex information and have only the information I need, when I need it. That enables me to make strategic choices that generate space for more quality time in my life. Using my Projecteze Table daily, I clear the clutter from my head so I can be more present and relaxed.

My greatest hope is that by using Projecteze you too will be able to maintain a balance between being efficient in your work and having quality time for yourself and the important relationships in your life.

# *II*

## Setting Up Your Projecteze Table

*By changing how you organize and share what you know,
you'll spend a lot less time on the things that don't matter
and a lot more time on the things that do.*
–Bill Jensen

Now that I've explained the rationale behind the system, it's time to show you how to work with a Projecteze Table and begin using the ultimate organizational system. I designed this book and my courses to help anyone with access to a computer and MS Word to get up and running with Projecteze within a couple of hours.

In this chapter, and on the assumption you are already somewhat familiar with MS Word, I will walk you through a description of how to set up your Projecteze Table. **You can start by downloading the template of a blank Projecteze Table that is already prepared for you from the website www. OnTopOfEverything.com.** Appendix A contains MS Word conversion tables for basic Projecteze procedures. A more detailed description of how to set up, format and work with your Projecteze Table is included in Appendices B and C. Appendix D contains a summary of menu equivalents between versions of MS Word.

Before you start using the Projecteze system, it is essential you become familiar with the recommended structure. **Even with the blank pre-formatted Projecteze Table from the website, it will be important for you to read through the remainder of this chapter so you understand the rationale behind the structure of the Projecteze Table and how to use it.**

After showing you how a Projecteze Table is set up, I will go over each component and describe how it functions. Next, I will show you how to name, save, archive and protect your table. By following a concrete illustration of how I use this system to manage a house construction project, you will come to appreciate the power of the sorting feature that animates every Projecteze Table.

Laurence Seton © | Projecteze Inc.

## Structure of the Projecteze Table

The simplicity and flexibility of the Projecteze system are two of its primary assets—ones that will ensure it continues to be a very powerful tool for you in organizing your projects and priorities. You are in the driver's seat; you decide what information to include in your table. With the Projecteze method, I'll show you how to manage information using features included in MS Word. This is what your Projecteze Table will look like before you populate it with information. "Prty" stands for Priority.

| Project | Date | Prty | Commitments & Action Items |
|---------|------|------|----------------------------|
|         |      |      |                            |
|         |      |      |                            |
|         |      |      |                            |
|         |      |      |                            |
|         |      |      |                            |

Note that the table shown above is proportionately correct. It looks smaller on a narrow page like this one, but on an 8.5" x 11" page with portrait orientation, it is wider, very easy to read, and looks great.

The font that is used is Times New Roman, 10 point, because it is one of the easiest fonts to read and it uses less space than most other fonts. [See instructions in Appendix E for how to change the default font for your MS Word documents.]

If you need to add another row to your Projecteze Table, this is a very simple process. Place your cursor inside the bottom right cell of your table (bottom row, furthest column to the right) and hit your *Tab* key. Presto! A new row appears for you to add information pertaining to that new project you were just handed.

Alternatively, you can add blank rows by:
- Using *Table>Insert>Rows Above* or *Rows Below;* or
- Placing your cursor just outside your table, on the right side of the row. Hit *Enter* and a new blank row will be created below that row.

## A Brief Description of Each Column

*The good news about computers*
*is that they do what you tell them to do.*
*The bad news is that they do what you tell them to do.*
−Ted Nelson

### Project

Use this column to enter the names of different projects, portions of projects, or personal initiatives. Later I will describe why you might want to divide a project into parts that would each occupy a discrete row.

A variation on this approach could be to assign a different group or discipline involved on a project to each row. This might be practical if you are managing one large project with input from several different disciplines or groups. For example, on an engineering design project, your rows could be assigned titles such as Mechanical, Electrical and Civil. This is where the flexibility of the Projecteze system starts to show itself. You design your table to fit your own needs.

### Date

Though seemingly self-explanatory, this is *one of the most important columns in your table*. The Date column drives the whole table and helps you stay on top of everything. You will enter a date in this column that corresponds to the next most immediate item in your Commitments & Action Items column, for each row. **You will only have one date in this column for each row.**

When you sort by the Date column, your table will reorganize itself so that the most pressing action rows appear at the top of the table−front and centre for you to view. Any rows that have a later action date will be sorted downward in the table and moved away from your main focus. You won't need to deal with those rows before you deal with the top rows, so this process gets them out of your way until they naturally rise to the top of the table.

Laurence Seton © | Projecteze Inc.

Those later dated rows will bubble to the top of your table when they warrant your attention.

MS Word will automatically recognize many different date formats, using the month (m), day (d) and year (y). I suggest you use the most simple format: "mmm d" (Jan 1) and "mmm dd" (Jan 10), if your dates are all within the current calendar year. For dates that extend beyond the current calendar year, use "mmm dd/yy" (Jan 15/12).

The "mmm d" (Jan 1) format can be used up until the ninth day of a month, and then when you need two digit dates, it can be expanded to "mmm dd" (Jan 10). You do not need to use "Jan 09". In this way, MS Word will allow you to write the date as you normally would, be it a one- or two-digit date.

With a date in every row of your table, MS Word automatically knows that column represents dates and will sort it as dates. *It is important that the top row in your Projecteze Table always have a date in the Date column.* Without a date in the top row, MS Word gets confused unless you tell it this is a date column *during* the sort process—which is an extra step that can be avoided simply by not having any blank rows in your table.

If the Date column for *any* row in the table is left blank, and the table is sorted by date, MS Word will move that row to the top of the table. To avoid running into this problem, do not have any completely blank rows in your table and *enter a date in the Date column for every row in your table.* As you become more familiar with the Projecteze Table, you'll notice that leaving a date out of the Date column will seem unnatural and feel like something is missing.

*Priority (Prty)*

The Priority column enables you to assign a priority to each of your rows, pertaining to the next commitment/action item for the row, and provides a secondary sorting capability for all the rows that bubble to the top of your table with the same date. As with the Date column, **you will only have one priority number in this column for each row.**

If you have several rows with the same date in the Date column, the secondary sort by Priority will cause the rows for that date to fall out in order of decreasing priority. This means that when you have sorted the table, the most immediate and highest priority action item(s) will be at the very top of your table.

Set the priority in the Prty column according to the priority of the next commitment/action item in that row. When you assign a priority level to a row, use a scale of only a few numbers such as 1, 2 or 3. Assign 1 to the highest priority rows and 3 to the lowest. Keep it simple.

I recommend that you use the abbreviation Prty for the title to this column in order to keep the column as narrow as possible, leaving more room for the Commitments & Action Items column.

*Commitments & Action Items*

This is where you will enter the majority of information about commitments, targets, and action items for each project (row). In this column and for each row (denoting a project or sub-project or topic), I recommend that you enter only the critical and most important information that *you* need to be aware of in order for *you* to stay on top of *your* work and projects.

Limit the amount of information you enter into this column to just enough to remind you what needs to be done, by whom, when, and perhaps, where the commitment was made or where you have filed additional reference documents. This might sound like a lot of information but it can usually all be captured as a one- or two-line item within this column. I will show you specific examples in the next chapter.

At the heart of the Commitments & Action Items column is a simple three-part formula for what I call "information packets":

- the next action date:

- a description of the commitment or action item

- the reference date and source in brackets.

As you capture and enter several items into the Commitments & Action Items column of a row, the row will automatically expand to look something like this:

- Date (for the most immediate commitment or action item to be completed—at the top) followed by a : (colon). A brief description of this most pressing commitment or action item for this project, including what was committed to, by whom, and the timing. Include commitments you have made or others have made to you. (In brackets, record the date the commitment was made and perhaps how (the source; meeting, email, etc), a description of pertinent reference documents such as a set of minutes or an email, and where you have stored those documents if you think you might need to access them again in the future).

- Date (for the second highest priority or chronologically timed item): as above.

- Date (for the third highest priority or chronologically timed item): as above.

- Add additional details important for tracking on this project such as items you want to capture for discussion and approval at the next project meeting with the client or a list of key dates pulled from the project schedule.

- Any other information you need to keep track of and have easily accessible.

Note that *each* information packet in the Commitments & Action Items column begins with a • or bullet. Make a habit of using bullets in front of each item you enter in the fourth column. As the list of commitments and action items in a row becomes longer, a bullet and a hanging indent will help to separate individual information packets and make them easier to scan. This will enable you to mentally process the information in your table more quickly.

I recommend that you insert bullets rather than use automated bullets because they use less space, and it's easy to do. To add bullets that will help your text stand out nicely using a shortcut key, follow these steps:

a) Menus *Insert>Symbol.*
b) Set the font to *Symbol.*
c) Type 0183 in the Character Code field, *Enter.*

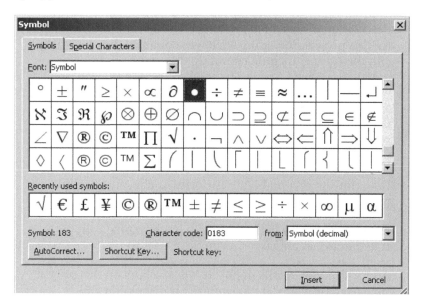

d) Click the *Shortcut Key* button.

e) With the cursor in the *Press new shortcut key*: press Ctrl + 0 (i.e. while holding down the Control key, press the zero key once).

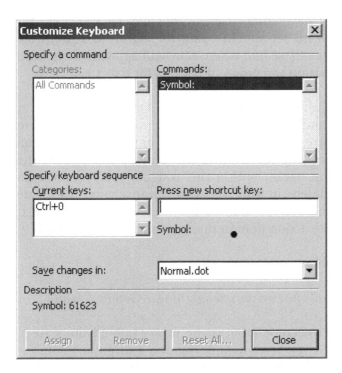

f.) Click *Assign* and *Close*

Now simply press *Ctrl+0* to add the • as you type.
(Mac® users: Option + 8 inserts a bullet in Times New Roman and most other fonts.)

g.) Add a hanging indent for the entire Commitments & Action Items column for better presentation and easier readability. The blank Projecteze Table from the website is already formatted with a hanging indent.
(See items 53 and 54 of Appendix C on page 175 for a detailed description of how to do this.)

You will have many such bulleted information packets in your Commitments & Action Items column for each row. They should be organized within a row in order of ascending date or descending priority. The action item with the most immediate date or highest priority should be at the top.

You will likely have some packets that describe an item for which there is no set specific date for action or resolution. Simply sequence these into where they will approximately need to take place within the group of packets for that row.

A key point to reinforce again is that the date you put into your Date column and the priority you put into your Prty column should both correspond to your next most immediate action item in the Commitments & Action Items column for that row—the top information packet within this row. As you complete an action item, delete it from the row. Then change the Date column and the Prty column so they correlate with the next most immediate action item in that row, and re-sort your table.

### Sorting the Table

*Electricity is really just organized lightning.* –George Carlin

Sorting your Projecteze Table is the power behind the system. Sorting enables you to move information and projects into or out of your field of focus as you need it—by project number, date, priority or any other parameter you choose.

Sorting an MS Word table is easy. With your cursor anywhere in the table, you can use the pull down *Table* menu and select *Sort*. A sort box pops open enabling you to sort by up to three parameters during one sort operation. You should see a pull-down list of your column headings for each sort option—enabling you to sort the table by the columns you select and in the order you select them.

Here's an important tip. If, prior to accessing the sort box, your cursor is not a single flashing cursor inside the table, but instead highlights text (even one single space or character), the sort box will give you a *Paragraphs* sort option. [See the screen shot on page 118.] This indicates that it thinks you want to sort just the text selected and not the entire table. If you have the *Paragraphs* option showing up, cancel the sort box, re-set your cursor any-where inside the table so it is a single flashing vertical line and go back to *Table>Sort*.

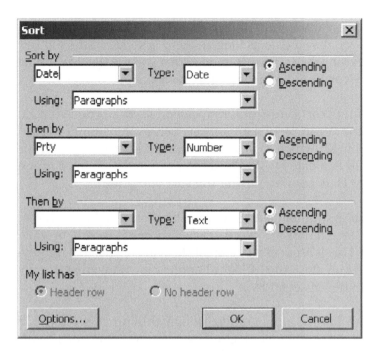

The flexibility of the Projecteze system shows itself here again. You can choose to sort by any of the columns in your table, and then just as easily re-sort it using another column or configuration.

The most powerful sort is by *Date* and *Prty* during the same sort operation, with both chosen as *Ascending*. By sorting with *Date-Prty (Ascending)*, your Projecteze Table will be put in order of the rows with the next most immediate date being at the top of the table, starting with the highest priority for that date. This brings the most pressing or urgent items to the top of your table for you to focus on immediately.

Remember, if you have any rows that are blank, anywhere in your Projecteze Table, and you sort the table, the blank rows will be brought to the top—which can interfere with MS Word recognizing the Date column for subsequent sorts. I recommend that you have only enough rows in the table as you need and that you put values in every row for the columns you will be sorting by.

Even if you use a "mmm-d" format (e.g. Apr 5), MS Word will automatically see it as a date as long as there is a date in the top row prior to starting the sort. I recommend that you use the date format in the way you would normally write, such as Apr 5 or Apr 17.

If you want to sort across different calendar years, you will need to use a more complete date format such as the "mmm dd/yy" (i.e. Jan 15/12) which falls nicely into the Date column and is recognized as a date by MS Word (no need to define the column as being a Date column during the sort operation).

When you first update and sort your Projecteze Table each day, you will have to tell MS Word that you want it to sort by Date and Prty. This is a necessary step at the start of each day or anytime after you close the MS Word application altogether. It only takes a matter of seconds.

Here's the bonus: after going through this process once, MS Word will remember your choices whenever you open your Projecteze document again, as long as you haven't closed the MS Word application in the meantime. You can close your Projecteze Table (the document) but minimize MS Word (the application) so it tucks down and out of the way until you need it. When you open your Projecteze Table again and make changes to it, the sort feature will still remember what your choices were for columns to sort by.

## Naming and Saving Your Table

The process for naming and saving your Projecteze Table is a fundamental aspect of the Projecteze method. Save your Projecteze Table using the following file naming convention: *Your initial&lastname-yyyy-mm-dd* (e.g. LSeton-2009-11-05)

This personalizes the table as being yours and makes it date specific.

Why do I want you to get in the habit of saving your Projecteze Table in this manner? Your Projecteze Table will be a living document. It will change every time you access it and add, delete or re-sort information. You could work with the same single, evolving copy of your Projecteze Table for months on end, but this would reduce the value of the Projecteze method. While common sense and prudence suggests you create a fail-proof backup system for any work you do with a computer, saving and archiving your table with a new name every day—just in case the version you are working on accidentally becomes corrupted or is deleted—is more than simply prudent; it is an essential part of the Projecteze method of organization.

Here's how it works.

At the beginning of your day, open your Projecteze Table from the previous day and, using this naming format based on date, save it as a new document with the new (current) date in the title.

You simply open your most recent table, select *File>Save As* and re-save the file —renaming it with the new date in the file name. Always use two digits for the "dd" (that day's date) portion of the name so that your documents will appear in chronological order when viewed by name. As an example, in the morning of Nov 6, I will re-save "LSeton-2009-11-05" to "LSeton-2009-11-06" quickly and easily by changing only one digit.

By saving your Projecteze document first thing each day with the current date in the document name, you will never have to experience losing all the hard work you have put into your Projecteze Table.

You might also want to consider inserting the *Page* and *Date* fields into the header of the page (*Insert>Field>Page* and *Date*). This Date field will be updated automatically to the current date every time you open the document. This is helpful because a printed hard copy will confirm what day the table pertains to. When you incorporate this feature, it makes having the current date in the document name essential.

The benefits of following my recommendations for naming and saving your Projecteze Table are:

• By re-naming your Projecteze document with the current date, each day you create a record of what were high priority commitments and action items for you over a period of days, weeks, months and years. These MS Word documents do not take up much computer storage space, and with your Projecteze Tables re-dated and saved every day, you create historical records that you can search, should the need arise, to find specific days or weeks when an action item was completed. Occasionally I've had the need to retrace my steps, and knowing the approximate time frame when something happened, it has taken me very little time to find the Projecteze document for the exact date that confirmed the timing of the event.

• If you accidentally delete some critical information in your Projecteze document, you will be able to restore most of this information by opening the Projecteze document from the previous day, then copying and pasting the missing information back into your current table.

• The sequence of documents in your Projecteze folder will fall nicely in chronological order when viewed by name— i.e. the bottom version will always be your most current, as long as you stick to using the naming format: *Your initial&lastname-yyyy-mm-dd.*

• In case you have to track down a Projecteze Table for a specific date, the creation date of all your archived versions will be easy to see when viewed by name.

Note that because the Date field in the header will automatically be updated when I open an older Projecteze document, *I will rely on the date contained in the name of the document* to confirm what date each document pertains to.

Once you get into the habit of saving and archiving your Projecteze Table daily, you won't have to worry about losing your information or having to re-build your Projecteze Table from scratch.

### Archiving Your Projecteze Table

I recommend that you set up a special folder for all of your Projecteze documents, preferably on a network drive that gets backed-up regularly. Name it whatever you choose. Once you set up this folder, add another folder inside it called *Archive*. Every so often move several of your previously dated Projecteze Tables from the main folder and into the nested Archive folder; this keeps your main folder uncluttered and makes it easy to find your table from the previous day.

I transfer all of my Projecteze Tables that are more than one week old into the Archive folder. By doing this, the window in my primary folder shows no more than the five most recent copies of my table—and therefore it's easy for me to find the most current version when I start my day.

It is equally important for you to save back-ups of your Projecteze documents and store them outside of your computer—regularly, if not daily. Most office environments provide automatic back-ups of documents that are saved to servers on the network. If you are saving your Projecteze documents only on your own computer, you could very well lose them all if the hard drive crashes.

If your office is not connected to a network server, you should habitually and regularly back up your Projecteze documents onto storage devices such as an external hard drive, a flash drive, burn them onto a CD or DVD, or use one of the many excellent on-line back-up services available. Your Projecteze documents will require very little storage space.

## Password Protection For Your Projecteze Table

When you first save your Projecteze Table, I recommend you add password protection for opening the document. This enables you to keep your Projecteze document personal and private so you can write whatever you want in it without having to be concerned about the possibility of other people scrutinizing your table. As little as a single keystroke can be used for a password—just don't forget what it is! See Appendix A on page 164 for the description of how to do this.

After you assign a password to your table the first time, you won't have to do it again because once you password-protect your current Projecteze document, it will automatically retain this password when you open and re-save it the following day with the new date in the document name. The only time you will need to consider changing your password is if you suspect someone else might know what it is and you want to maintain limited access.

With the password protection, you can save your Projecteze document into a folder on a network server and still retain privacy with the comfort of knowing back-ups are being performed automatically.

## Using Your Projecteze Table—An Illustrated Example

*Warning: Dates on calendar are closer than they appear.*
—Anonymous

Now that you've got your table set up, let's take a look at how you can use it. This is my favorite part of the book because it's likely to be when you have the most "Aha!" experiences as you begin to understand just how powerful this method is.

The example I will use here is for the construction of a house. You can simply read this example, but you might find it more helpful if you work with me and enter the same information into your own table so that you can have a hands-on experience of how to sort and manipulate information. That way, you will come to better understand the flexibility this system provides and how it can be reconfigured to your heart's delight and in ways that best suit your own needs.

*Populating The First Three Columns In Your Projecteze Table*

Building a house could be viewed as a single project, however, we all know that because of the complexity of the endeavor, it has several stages or sub-projects, involving different people and a variety of interdependent timelines. The opportunities for forgetting information or having conflicting events are easy to imagine. A Projecteze Table can help you stay completely on top of a project like this.

a) First, I would like you to enter the following sub-project descriptions of house construction stages into your table, one into the first column of each of the six blank rows under the header row:

- Design
- Concrete Foundation
- Framing
- Enclosure
- Interior
- Completion

| Project | Date | Prty | Commitments & Action Items |
|---------|------|------|---------------------------|
| Design | | | |
| Concrete Foundation | | | |
| Framing | | | |
| Enclosure | | | |
| Interior | | | |
| Completion | | | |

Notice how if the text is longer than the column is wide, it will wrap around to the next line within that cell. MS Word does this automatically within tables.

b) Now enter the following dates in the second (Date) column of the table, corresponding to each of the six stages you just entered. These represent the anticipated dates each of the stages will begin:

- Jan 10
- Apr 5
- May 15
- June 15
- July 15
- Sept 25

In other words, they are the next most immediate action date for each stage. Normally, you would add this information in the Date column after evaluating the information in the Commitments & Action Items column, but for setting up this example, I have looked ahead and am providing them to you now.

c) Enter a priority of "2" into each row for the Prty column. The priority of each row will change as the project unfolds and as the next most immediate action item in each row takes on a higher or lower priority. Your table should now look like this:

| Project | Date | Prty | Commitments & Action Items |
|---|---|---|---|
| Design | Jan 10 | 2 | |
| Concrete Foundation | Apr 5 | 2 | |
| Framing | May 15 | 2 | |
| Enclosure | June 15 | 2 | |
| Interior | July 15 | 2 | |
| Completion | Sept 25 | 2 | |

Laurence Seton © | Projecteze Inc.

*Populating The Fourth Column*

The fourth column, Commitments & Action Items, is where key information will be entered. As you use the Projecteze system, you will learn how you can alter both the type of information and level of detail entered in the fourth column to what best suits your own needs.

For this example, enter the following information, using the bullets shortcut keystroke of *Ctrl+0*, all into the fourth column for each designated row. I have assigned dates to items that will occur in the near future. Items that do not have a date associated with them are included as tasks that will have to be completed at some time during the construction of the house but which are not required just yet; we simply know that they are part of the project and will have to be sequenced and coordinated (dated) in the future as the house construction proceeds:

Design
* Jan 10 mtg with architect: Cover design preferences, timing, design fees & next steps
* Review design draft with architect
* Select materials and colors
* Sign-off on finalized design
* Drawings prepared for construction

Concrete Foundation
* Footings poured
* Forms for basement walls placed
* Walls poured

Framing
* Floor joists and plywood installed
* Pre-framed walls received and erected
* Roof joists installed

Enclosure
* Roofing installed
* Exterior siding installed
* Interior drywall installed

Interior
- Plumbing installed
- Electrical wiring installed
- Kitchen cabinets installed
- Other fixtures installed
- Lighting installed

Completion
- Sept 25: Targeted house completion

Now your completed table should look like this:

| Project | Date | Prty | Commitments & Action Items |
|---------|------|------|----------------------------|
| **Design** | Jan 10 | 2 | • Jan 10 mtg with architect: Cover design preferences, timing, design fees & next steps<br>• Review design draft with architect<br>• Select materials and colors<br>• Sign-off on finalized design<br>• Drawings prepared for construction |
| **Concrete Foundation** | Apr 5 | 2 | • Footings poured<br>• Forms for basement walls placed<br>• Walls poured |
| **Framing** | May 15 | 2 | • Floor joists and plywood installed<br>• Pre-framed walls received and erected<br>• Roof joists installed |
| **Enclosure** | June 15 | 2 | • Roofing installed<br>• Exterior siding installed<br>• Interior drywall installed |
| **Interior** | July 15 | 2 | • Plumbing installed<br>• Electrical wiring installed<br>• Kitchen cabinets installed<br>• Other fixtures installed<br>• Lighting installed |
| **Completion** | Sept 25 | 2 | • Sept 25: Targeted house completion |

*Notice that in the process of building the table and to provide an easier starting point, I have already sequenced the rows in order of next most immediate action date in the Date column.*

As you continue to work with Projecteze Tables, you will see how the hanging indent in the Commitments & Action Items column improves the presentation and readability of information.

*Putting The Projecteze Table To Work For You*

Remember that your Projecteze Table is a *living document*. What we've created so far is a nice breakdown of basic tasks to be completed for taking a new house from a dream to a reality. Now it's time to align that table with what is happening for the building of this house in real time.

Let's continue with our example and show how the Projecteze Table works for you as the project progresses and unexpected changes happen.

Looking at the top row of the table, you'll see I have listed items I need to discuss with the architect in a future meeting on Jan 10th.

Let's assume that a few days have passed, that we've had our Jan 10th meeting with the architect and all is proceeding well. In our Jan 10th meeting with the architect, we set a date of Jan 25th for the next meeting to review an initial draft of the house design.

Then suddenly, on Jan 15th, we get a call from the architect who tells us the type of lighting fixture we want, the only one we said we would settle for, has a delivery time of seven months—which is just about all the time we have left before our targeted completion date for the house. The architect tells us that we can't wait and we will have to order the lighting ourselves—as soon as possible.

The architect provides us with a telephone number and a contact name for the supplier, Jim Brown. We call and speak with Jim to arrange a meeting as soon as possible to confirm the fixtures model number, color, quantity, and pay him a deposit. He is available to meet on Jan 17th.

On Jan 15th after making the appropriate changes in the

Projecteze Table and re-sorting, it looks like this:

| Project | Date | Prty | Commitments & Action Items |
|---|---|---|---|
| Interior | Jan 17 | 1 | • Jan 17: Meeting with Jim Brown, Best Lighting (261-7522) re: order fixtures and pay deposit (Jan 15)<br>• Plumbing installed<br>• Electrical wiring installed<br>• Kitchen cabinets installed<br>• Other fixtures installed<br>• Lighting installed |
| Design | Jan 25 | 2 | • Jan 25: Review design draft with architect (Jan 10 mtg)<br>• Select materials and colors<br>• Sign-off on finalized design<br>• Drawings prepared for construction |
| Concrete Foundation | Apr 5 | 2 | • Footings poured<br>• Forms for basement walls placed<br>• Walls poured |
| Framing | May 15 | 2 | • Floor joists and plywood installed<br>• Pre-framed walls received and erected<br>• Roof joists installed |
| Enclosure | June 15 | 2 | • Roofing installed<br>• Exterior siding installed<br>• Interior drywall installed |
| Completion | Sept 25 | 2 | • Sept 25: Targeted house completion |

Can you see the changes I made to the Projecteze Table? Here's how I did it:

• First I deleted the reference to the Jan 10th meeting with the architect from the Design row because that has already taken place and I no longer need to track it.

• Because I have already set the date for my next meeting with the architect, I've added that date, Jan 25th, to the front of the action item "Review design draft with architect" in the Design row, added a reference to our Jan 10th meeting in brackets at the end and changed the date in the Date column to Jan 25th. I made this change because that is the *next most immediate date pertaining to that row*. In other words, the date in the Date column acts like a flag telling us that on Jan 25th—and not until then—something on that row will have to be dealt with.

- Then I added a description of the Jan 17th meeting with the lighting fixtures supplier in the "Interior" row, at the top of the Commitments & Action Items for this row because it will be the next most immediate action I will have to take for the Interior sub-project.

- Then I added the date Jan 17th in front of the description of this action item *and* in the Date column for the Interior row (again, the next most immediate date for an action item in this row).

- Then I raised the Priority for the Interior row to a 1 to reflect the urgency of ordering those light fixtures as soon as possible.

- Then I re-sorted the table by "Date" and "Prty", both during a single sort operation.

Try to follow these steps as you modify your own table until it looks the same as the one shown above.

**The Power of Sorting**

*Time is what keeps things from happening all at once.*
—James Archibald Wheeler

Let's take a look at why I made some of the changes I made to the table and you will understand how the Projecteze method of applying daily attention and updating your table regularly will keep you current and well organized.

Going back to the example above, I want to reinforce why I added the date Jan 17th to *both* the Date column and in front of the action item itself.

This is a critical step for using the Projecteze system and is the foundation for realizing the full power of it. Having a date in front of information packets in the fourth (Commitments & Action Items) column makes it easy to scan through them and identify what items warrant your immediate attention. Having a date in the second (Date) column that coincides with the earliest information packet date, from the fourth column, will bring rows with the most pressing issues to the top of your table and to the center of your attention when you sort the table by Date and Prty. In this way, you minimize the clutter in front of you as the less pressing, lower priority items will be sorted further down in the table and out of your way—for the time being.

Another benefit associated with inserting a date in front of as many packets as you can in the fourth column is that, with one glance, they help increase your awareness of future action items and commitments that are coming at you beyond the most immediate action item.

Rearranging the information packets in your Commitments & Action Items column within a row by action date is easy to do. Simply highlight a specific information packet (*click & drag across* to highlight or *three clicks of the mouse* will highlight the entire packet) and then drag it to its proper chronological place within that cell.

It is worth noting here that even with having the less pressing projects (rows) sorted downward and out of the way, it will become second nature for you to quickly scan a page or two ahead in your Projecteze Table to see what is coming at you further down the road. It takes very little time to do this and is often all you need as a reminder about future commitments and action items. And it's not difficult because your Projecteze Table can contain many projects and sub-projects within only a few pages.

Scanning through those dates and descriptions can help you to see the bigger picture for each project and sub-project. You'll be giving yourself a heads-up about items that are coming up over the next week or month to possibly help you recognize underlying patterns that could provide a better overall solution with greater leverage than if the items were dealt with individually or one at a time.

Laurence Seton © | Projecteze Inc.

When you update and re-sort your Projecteze Table at the end of the day (to get prepared for the following day), all items that warrant your more immediate attention on the following day will bubble up to or be near the top of your Projecteze Table.

*If any one row (project) in your Projecteze Table starts to exceed a full page in depth, you might want to consider inserting a new row and splitting the information from that one row into two, separating your packets into re-named rows for sub-projects that make logical sense.*

**Implications of Using Projecteze:**
**Clear Communication and Accountability**

*Give me ambiguity or give me something else.*
—Anonymous

Using a Projecteze Table will enhance your life and sense of organization in three ways. First, it promotes clear communication. Secondly, it enhances accountability—for you and for others working on the same project. And thirdly, it reinforces good project management techniques by requiring that you continually revisit and track your highest priorities.

Looking back at the table I used to illustrate how a Projecteze Table became a living document during house construction, you can see all three factors at work. Note that for the action item concerning the meeting with Jim Brown about the lighting, I also added his phone number and the date of our telephone conversation.

When you add the date and perhaps the form of communication in brackets at the end of the description (e.g. Jan 15 tel call), it acts as a reminder when and where the topic was discussed. You will come to appreciate just how helpful this can be when you're dealing with something that took place many weeks or months ago and bubbles to the top of your table one day. It is especially helpful when it involves a commitment that was made by someone else to you. You can also add a brief description of where you filed pertinent documents. This alone has saved me countless hours of searching for lost documents because my Projecteze Table told me exactly where I had put them.

For example, after our Jan 17th meeting with the lighting supplier, I will enter a new action item into the next iteration of my Projecteze Table telling me that during our meeting, Jim committed to having a confirmation to me by no later than Feb 1st of the lighting fixtures order having been placed. When I add this new Feb 1st action item to my table, I will set my next action date in the Date column to *Feb 2nd*, the day *after* Jim committed to having the confirmation to me. This gives Jim the entire day of Feb 1st to complete his commitment. When this row bubbles to the top of my table, on Feb 2nd, if I have received the confirmation from Jim by then, I simply delete this packet from my table. Gone. It is no longer pertinent because it was completed. Removing completed items from the table will keep it as clean and simple as possible with only the items that still matter remaining. And it is a very rewarding experience to be able to delete completed tasks. In this way, your Projecteze Table won't continue to grow indefinitely but will instead fluctuate in size as activities are added and deleted. *It truly is a living, breathing document.*

Let's say that on the morning of Feb 2nd and after reviewing my Projecteze Table for that day, I notice I have not yet received confirmation of the lighting fixtures order from Jim. I will call Jim early on Feb 2nd and calmly inquire: "Jim, in our meeting of Jan 17th, you said you would be able to have confirmation of my order over to me by Feb 1st. I haven't received it yet. When do you think you'll have it to me?"

Not only was I able to reference the meeting he made the commitment in, but I mentioned the exact date as well, simply reiterating the commitment Jim made to me at that time. I was following up on his commitment—the day after it was due.

Why is this important?

The squeaky wheel gets the grease. If I'm building a house and

Jim is having a busy year, I want to make sure I do everything I possibly can to help move the process along for my own project. Again, politeness is the order of the day but I can't count how many times I've used this approach with positive and favorable results. Reciting the exact date the commitment was made to the person who made the commitment does several things:

- It makes it clear that they did in fact make the commitment and that you know that.

- It often quickly brings back into their memory exactly what you're talking about.

- It reminds them that this was their commitment to the date in the first place and not one you imposed upon them.

    Note: When setting dates to have something completed, I will usually ask the other person for their date first. When can they have it completed? If it's a good date for me, I'll agree to it. This date is from that point forward their date, not mine, a deadline which they have set for themselves and are obligated to live up to. If they miss this date, it can't get turned around into a complaint that I set an unrealistic date to begin with.

- It shows them that you are extremely well organized and on top of your projects. And it suggests that you aren't likely to go away until the commitment is met.

This is a wonderful way to be the squeaky wheel without ever having to raise your voice, get angry with anyone, or most importantly, to belittle anyone. It's a process of learning how to manage other people so they enjoy working with you and will respect you as being someone who is completely on top of their work—all the time.

So I do call Jim early on Feb 2nd and remind him of his commitment and ask him when he thinks he'll have the confirmation to me. He may have a really valid reason, not just an excuse, for having missed the date, and I want to give him a chance to share it with me. What ever it is, I want to hear it. If it's just because he dropped the ball or forgot about it, I'm doing us both a favor by reminding him about it. Nine times out of ten, the response I get will be a valid reason but with the additional commitment that I will have what I was originally promised very soon. It more often than not gets sorted out very amicably and very quickly, and this keeps my project on track.

For any row in my Projecteze Table, if I see a critical deliverable or commitment approaching that will take a long time to be completed, I might set my flag date in the Date column to the mid-point of that duration with a note to myself to check in with the other person, just to see how it's coming along. This helps to keep the "Oh, I forgot all about it!" surprises at the deadline to a minimum.

Using the Projecteze system in this way is instrumental for minimizing emotional reactions by yourself or others you're talking to. Being on top of everything along with an understanding attitude goes a long way toward fostering harmonious relationships with the people you have to deal with.

# Just The Right Level Of Detail

*Simplicity is the ultimate sophistication.*
—Leonardo da Vinci

The Projecteze system is simple yet sophisticated. It's simple because it uses common software to manage your key commitments from all of your projects in a single, centralized location. It's sophisticated because it provides a systematic way for you to organize, prioritize and flag action items in advance—bringing them forward into your field of focus only when you need to deal with them. Leonardo would have loved it.

Occasionally when I have been managing projects, it felt as though I wasn't making much progress on one or two of them, but after consulting my own Projecteze Table, I always knew I was focused on the most important issues at all times. This was very reassuring. My Projecteze Table helped me make sure I stayed on track and didn't get pulled away on some tangent or whim—which would have scattered my energy and distracted me. Looking back, I know that I gained the maximum benefit for every effort I exerted.

In this chapter I will show you three techniques you can use to adjust the level of detail in your Projecteze Table and gain greater efficiency in organizing your work and home life.

Laurence Seton © | Projecteze Inc.

## Adjusting the Level of Detail: Essentials and Efficiency

*I took a speed-reading course*
*and read War and Peace in twenty minutes.*
*It involves Russia.*
−Woody Allen

Projecteze enhances your ability to see projects from a broader perspective and to recognize new ideas or solutions that could have a much greater leverage and impact on the overall success of your work. The key to keeping your Projecteze Table functioning at the highest level is to populate it with information expressed as economically as possible and yet with just enough detail to provide all the dimensions you need to keep moving forward with all your commitments and action items.

In this section, I will suggest how to customize your Projecteze Table so that the document can really come to life. I will show you how to regulate the level of detail to be included for each project (row) in your table. This is where some of the Projecteze method's greatest value lies: a concept for you to keep in mind as you work with and develop your Projecteze Table is to "keep it simple" by recording only essential information. This will prevent information overload and will promote the greatest ease of use.

## Capturing Information

During our workdays, each of us uses a different method for capturing important information pertaining to our projects, tasks and schedules. Some of you may use project notebooks, file folders, or calendars, or even the ubiquitous sticky notes to record ideas emerging from your interactions throughout the day. Your written notes capture critical items for tracking and follow-up on issues stemming from telephone conversations, emails, and meeting minutes. Other information will flow to you in the form of specific documents such as schedules, cost reports, and project progress reports. Some of these items will be in hard copy, others will be electronic.

Whatever your method of recording notes, your Projecteze Table will become the ultimate destination for key information. With this system, your payoff will be that you never have to look back through your notes beyond the current day. You will either have dealt with action items already—or have captured them in your Projecteze Table. It is very liberating to not have to flip back through pages and pages in your notebook to see if you've addressed everything. As you transfer key commitments and action items into your table, it becomes the single, centralized location of information for all your projects, the foundation for all your work.

With the goal of helping you increase your efficiency and effectiveness, I'm including a detailed explanation of how to process information because I believe it will help you identify and extract the most important details from all the documents and events that fill your typical workday. Here are a few suggestions that will help you capture and process vital information.

As you record important commitments and action items in your *notebook*, I suggest you put a small bullet point in front of each new item in order to make it more easily identifiable as separate from other items. (Visually, this is similar to how I recommended you enter information packets into your Projecteze Table.) During or at the end of each exchange or meeting, **draw a large circle around the bullet of the items that directly affect you and will require action or follow-up by you**—which is often in the form of a commitment from you or by someone else to you.

The following shows one example of each. I have recorded the first item in my notebook as general information. It does not need to be included in my Projecteze Table. The second item affects me directly so I highlight it for capture in my table by circling the bullet point.

- Project Execution Plan will be with the client for review for next 2 weeks.

⊙ Feb 15: Report due from John for my editing and distribution.

At some point in time during the day, you will need to either act on the items you circled or capture them in your Projecteze Table for action in the future. In my work, if it's a five-minute item, I'll try to take care of it at my earliest opportunity. If it's going to take longer than that, I'll transfer it as an action item into my Projecteze Table so it can be prioritized appropriately.

As soon as a short duration item has been completed or an item has been recorded into my Projecteze Table for future action, I return to my notebook and put a check mark through the large circle surrounding the bullet for that item. Then it will look like this.

 Feb 15: Report due from John for my editing and distribution.

A quick scan of my notebook confirms I've either dealt with or captured everything important in my Projecteze Table.

When I'm in a meeting, I make notes about the commitments I have made and the commitments others have made that directly affect me. Before the end of the day, I make sure I transfer the items that have not been completed into my Projecteze Table.

When I receive minutes from a meeting, I'll scan through them to make sure I've captured in my table all the pertinent commitments and action items that involve me. Then I file the minutes and only refer to them should something come up in the future that requires a greater understanding of the details discussed in that meeting. Otherwise, I don't look at them again because the most pertinent information for me is captured in my Projecteze Table.

## Your Projecteze Table May Flow Onto Many Pages

*Stress is when you wake up screaming
and you realize you weren't sleeping.*
—Anonymous

As you add only essential information into the Commitments &
Action Items column for each project or row, your Projecteze
Table will automatically expand downward. This is normal and
another great feature of MS Word. It is also not unusual for
the initial set-up and refining of your Projecteze Table to take
several hours. Once you have populated your table, don't be sur-
prised if your entire document grows to three or five pages—
that is not unusual. Just be assured your table will still be very
easy to manage and use. After you sort it, the first one or two
pages will be the ones that show items for your current attention. This makes it easy to scan across the more urgent issues
very quickly with the other less pressing or future project items
out of your way.

The Projecteze Table is formatted to *Allow rows to break across
pages* (found by going to *Table>Table Properties>Row*). This
means that any row in your table can flow over the page and
onto the next page should it expand and exceed the space available on the current page. (The entire row doesn't shift; a portion
of that row will flow over onto the following page.)

The blank Projecteze Table you downloaded from the website
www.OnTopOfEverything.com has been formatted to keep your
table contiguous and flowing smoothly from one page to another.
However, occasionally a row might not flow smoothly onto the
next page and instead shift as an entire unit, leaving a large gap
between rows where you wouldn't think it necessary. Fear not
because your Projecteze Table is still very much intact, well
organized, and in the sequence you need it. If, as your
Projecteze Table expands and after a re-sort, gaps like this do
show up between rows, go to the Downloads page of the website
and read "Setting Page Breaks In Your Projecteze Table". It
describes how to re-set "Paragraph Formatting" to avoid this.

## Commitments & Action Items–Information Per Row

*Vital papers will demonstrate their vitality*
*by moving from where you left them*
*to where you can't find them.*
–Anonymous

If you end up putting extensive lists of details into your Projecteze Table, it will start to look like any other "To Do List" that is not only huge but also overwhelming, de-motivating, and completely useless.

Instead, enter brief notes concerning critical details that you need to remember or quickly access. These notes will trigger your memory and can include succinct details to remind you where to find supporting documents or additional information.

You will recall from the last chapter, that the heart of the Projecteze system is based on the following three-part configuration for each information packet entered into the Commitments & Action Items column:

> • The next date that action on this item is to be taken: a description of the commitment and/or action item using what, who, and when, including commitments you have made or others have made to you (in brackets, the date the commitment was made, when and perhaps where supporting documents have been filed).

Sometimes you will see an item come up in your table that you added several weeks earlier. A quick read will remind you what the action item is and when the commitment was made (in brackets at the end of the packet). Should you need to remind yourself about specific details, the description of where you stored the original documents will enable you to find them quickly for review.

An example of information packets in the Commitments & Action column might look like this:

---

- July 19: Have I received a list of deliverables from all Discipline Leads for their scope of work? (requested July 2 Project Mtg).

- Dave asked to pursue 5-yr renewal next year with termination clause after 18 months; Bill asked to respond with any concerns he has with this approach (July 11 emails; see File-365 for originals).

- July 20: Steve to confirm next step for construction financing and approval (July 17 call).

- July 20: Warren to send me Request For Services; work to be done by end of Aug (July 12).

- Aug 2: Issue P.O. for arena renovations; funding approval due at Aug 1 Council Mtg.

- Aug 30: Mary to provide cost centre & EOC for OE's & rent to end of the fiscal year, for budget transfer (July 18).

---

Notice that for one of the above entries, there is no date in front of the information packet. The date can be left out for action items that are floaters—they don't have to be completed by a specific time. These might be issues or project details that you need to monitor but aren't as time sensitive or can only be dated after something else has been completed. Expect to have several of these non-dated but equally important descriptions or flags included in your table—just keep them brief and slot them in where they should be, in relation to the other packets.

## Commitments & Action Items–Open Flexibility

*Very funny Scotty. Now beam down my clothes.*
–Captain James T. Kirk

The ability to sort the Projecteze Table is a foundational strength of the system. The flexibility of what to include and how to structure information within the fourth column– Commitments & Action Items–is another key feature of the Projecteze system and one that needs to be reinforced.

The examples I have shown you above provide a good start for understanding how to structure information in the fourth column. The recommended configuration for information packets is based on years of experience. It works well and there is a tremendous flexibility for what type of information you can enter and how you enter it.

Chapter Two describes how to structure several information packets as well as other key details in the fourth column:

* Date (for the most immediate commitment or action item to be completed–at the top) followed by a : (colon). A brief description of this most pressing commitment or action item for this project, including what was committed to, by whom, and the timing. Include commitments you have made or others have made to you. (In brackets, note the date the commitment was made and perhaps how (the source; meeting, email, etc), a description of pertinent reference documents such as a set of minutes or an email, and where you have stored those documents if you think you might need to access them again in the future).

* Date (for the second highest priority or chronologically timed item): as above.

* Date (for the third highest priority or chronologically timed item): as above.

- Add additional details important for tracking on this project such as items you want to capture for discussion and approval at the next project meeting with the client or a list of key dates pulled from the project schedule.

- Any other information you need to keep track of and have easily accessible.

This is an excellent format to follow and you will find it works very well.

In Chapter Four (Projecteze For Work), you will see examples of where I placed a sequence of dates taken straight from a project schedule into my Projecteze Table for easy reference. The example looks like this:

- Set up a mtg with the Contractor for Bryan & me to get an understanding of why the tiles installation price was so high this year (see my email of April 20 to Bryan).

SCHEDULE: (May 3)
- June 3 – July 28: Station 25 renovation.
- June 28 – July 20: Station 14 renovation.
- July 1 – 30: Stations 11 & 12 tiles installation.
- July 4 & Aug 3 long weekends – tiles installation at Station 2.
- July 9 – 18: CALGARY STAMPEDE (no work to be done on any platforms).
- July 15: Are the Station 7 warranty repairs finished??
- July 19 – Aug 7: NE Leg platforms sealed.
- July 19 – Sept 13: Miscellaneous repairs at all stations.
- Jacob to collect keys and security passes from General Contractor at the end of construction.

Using this technique enables me to keep track of key dates on a project without having to refer to another document. As a project progresses and dates change, I can update them in my Projecteze Table quickly and easily because it is only the major milestones that I'm trying to keep track of. If I need greater detail about a specific schedule item, I will refer to the actual schedule. More often than not, and not needing to micro-manage my staff or contractors, this level of detail works very well for staying on top of a project.

I can also enter information I need to refer to often. This is a sample taken from my own Projecteze Table for the preparation of this book, in a row dedicated to "Book Publication". I found I frequently had to refer to the ISBN numbers for the book and this was a great place to have ready access to them:

- April 15: Update the ISBN re: when the book is going to be published; last updated Feb 20 for a June 10 publication date.
- June 15: Send two copies of book to CISS Depository; see instructions on website

- ISBNs: Soft cover:
  ISBN-13: 978-0-9810629-0-7 (9780981062907)
  ISBN-10: 0-9810629-0-3 (0981062903)
  (eBook: 978-0-9810629-1-4)

There is a lot of flexibility for how you can structure the information entered in the Commitments & Actions column. Three very important points to remember though are:

a) Enter only the level of detail *you* need to track items that impact you.

b) Sequence the information packets so the most pressing items are at the top of the row. Most will have dates assigned to them but some might not.

c) Enter other key reference information below the more critical or pressing items.

## Breaking Down Projects Into Many Rows

*Multi-tasking, when it comes to paying attention, is a myth.*
*We are biologically incapable*
*of processing attention-rich inputs simultaneously.*
–Dr. John Medina

So far, I've talked mostly about allocating each project or sub-project to a row. You might want to consider adding deeper levels of details to your Projecteze Table.

The flexibility of the Projecteze method allows you to decide when and how to break your projects up, and into whatever level of detail you require, by simply creating additional rows in your table.

The result is that you will be able to add rows to track "sub-projects" or "sub-sub-projects" for greater accuracy. As the need for a greater concentration on these sub-sub-projects decreases, you can re-combine the remaining commitments and action items back into a single higher-level row.

In the house-building illustration I showed you in Chapter Two, I broke the construction process into stages or sub-projects. I also had the freedom to take one of those sub-projects and break it down even further. This can be helpful if one stage of a project becomes overly full with commitments or action items, especially if many of them can be logically separated from the rest.

For example, in my Projecteze Table, I had one row designated as *Design* that pertained to the design of the house. As the construction progressed, I could have divided this category into more specific sub-projects such as House Design and Landscaping Design, especially because these construction items involve different contractors with discrete schedules. It would not be necessary to divide them if there were only a few tasks being added for the landscaping design, but if that aspect of the overall project became more complicated, I would benefit by putting it into a separate row. That would enable me to get the entire Landscaping Design row and all of its contents out of my way until I need it. The Projecteze method easily accommodates this kind of change without complicating either the table or where I need to place my focus.

# IV

## Projecteze For Work:
## Move Beyond Just Keeping Up

*You only need two tools in life—WD-40® and duct tape.*
*If it doesn't move and should, use the WD-40®.*
*If it shouldn't move and does, use the duct tape.*
—Anonymous

Today's workplace demands that you continually manage more and more information. With a steady and growing volume of information and paper that flows at us every day, it's a major challenge to simply keep up. Just the coordination of an average day's workload is a sizeable task in itself: there are meetings to attend, reports to write, phone calls to return, and projects to manage.

How well you do this has a direct impact on your success as an individual and, ultimately, how well your organization succeeds. Without a system to help you stay organized and on top of your responsibilities, you can be left behind the proverbial eight ball, staring at a mountain of work that simply continues to grow and grow.

Let's take a look at a typical situation for an average office employee.

Homer works for a custom manufacturer of highway trucks. He regularly gets into his office at 8:00 AM sharp, logs on to his computer, and opens his email. When he left work the night before, he'd read all of his emails. At that point, there were 2,258 old messages in his inbox.

From those emails, Homer knew he had several outstanding commitments to fulfill, so he made it a practice to continually review all of the emails he had received over the previous few days. At the rate of 25 to 40 emails a day, that meant he routinely scanned about 100 emails and re-read the ones that required his attention—looking for the next thing he had to do.

When Homer opened his email this morning, he saw five new emails. That's all. But two of those were from his boss, which usually meant he was going to have some extra work to do. True enough. Homer's manager advanced the deadline for a report that was due next week. Homer had to have it completed by noon, today! The second email from his boss directed Homer to take immediate action on a newly developing staff matter. The boss had flagged both items "high priority".

Homer's head began to spin. All of his previous "To Do" items

Laurence Seton © | Projecteze Inc.

left over from yesterday circled in his head as he crammed in these additional tasks from his boss. And he still had three more emails to open. Two were from co-workers–both jokes. ("Phew!") He'd have to check them out later. The last one was from his most important client who requested that Homer respond to some questions. No problem. The client didn't seem to be in a rush. All Homer knew was that he'd better not forget to respond to her today because he *did* forget to answer that same client's email last week and got reamed out royally.

Now Homer began to ask himself what he should do next. He was having enough trouble just keeping everything straight in his head, let alone deciding what action he should take first. And then, Homer received another email–from the Line Foreman– asking for clarification on an aspect of the vehicle assembly. This couldn't wait. The Line Foreman's question concerned a chassis that was halfway down the production line and he required an immediate answer.

All of a sudden Homer began to feel his necktie tighten. The tie didn't change, but Homer did. His blood pressure climbed and he had that sinking feeling in his stomach. His stress level elevated and his mouth went dry. And it was only 8:15 in the morning. "Go!" That's all Homer could think. "Do the truck chassis first." Off he went to find the answer for the Line Foreman. But on his way back to his desk, he ran into the accountant who needed some clarification on billing numbers. More demands; more pain. And so began Homer's day.

After a complete day of this, Homer was clearly spent, burned out and exhausted–as he is most days. And it was only Tuesday! Three more days to go before he would get that cherished weekend to himself. Ah, the weekend: two whole days without being stressed to the maximum–except that never happens because Homer will keep thinking about everything he failed to accomplish during the week and all the balls he dropped that will need to be cleaned up next week. Homer will remain a captive to his job–unless he decides to use a system that will help him get organized and back on top of everything.

Louise is Homer's co-worker. She uses the Projecteze system to stay on top of everything. Let's take a look into her day.

When Louise arrives at her desk in the morning, she starts off in much the same way as Homer. She logs on to her computer and opens her email. This is where the similarity ends. Louise also opens her Projecteze Table. She has populated the table with all her commitments and action items. Louise developed her table over the past month, applied the system every day, and now she's arrived at the point where it's really starting to pay off for her.

In her Projecteze Table, Louise has captured commitments she made to others, requests from her boss, other action items she must complete, and even commitments others have made to her so she can keep track of them. In addition to capturing all of these items, she has also noted the timing for each one.

She assimilated important dates and figures into her table: When her boss expects to have the third quarter sales report on his desk. When Sam in Parts is committed to getting information to her so she can include it in her sales report. By associating a date with each item, she has sequenced them for tracking, monitoring and completion. Nothing that impacts her work is missed or forgotten. And perhaps best of all, Louise has an accurate understanding of the priority for each item. Her Projecteze Table tells her what the highest priority and most urgent item is that she should be working on next. As an added bonus, her email inbox has very few emails in it. Louise doesn't have to search back through hundreds of old emails to remind her what needs to be done and this helps to keep her stress levels down.

Louise sees that she too has received five new emails that morning. Two are from her boss with requests for her attention. As Louise opens each of her boss's emails, she copies the text describing the request and pastes it right into her Projecteze Table. Having captured all of the information she needs to remind her what her boss has requested, she closes and files each email into a separate folder she has created for notes from her boss, removing them from her inbox.

She only has three emails left in her inbox. The next one is from a very important client, Filmore Logging, asking her to provide some answers before the end of the day. She makes a short note in her Projecteze Table: "Respond to Filmore questions (see email)" with the current date as a flag. Then she files that email into her Filmore Logging email folder. The last two emails are jokes from friends; she will check them out later.

At this point, Louise's email inbox is clear of action items. Everything she needs to know is captured in her Projecteze Table. Working with her table, she is able to easily click and drag the brief bulleted points within one row into a sequence by priority for that row. She can then sort the rows in her table by date and priority. After updating her table in this way and with a quick review of her entire table, she knows what all of her highest priorities are, exactly what action she needs to take first, whom it impacts, and where to find reference information in either electronic or hard copy.

Louise, like Homer, will experience interruptions and unexpected requests throughout her day, but when they come up, she can deal with them appropriately and with confidence. Louise is able to maintain a focus on her highest priority items at all times, and she won't allow a low priority interruption to interfere and drag her off on a tangent, potentially sabotaging her productivity and throwing her off course for the day. She will simply write them in her notebook and add them to her Projecteze Table as soon as she can. Then, when it's appropriate, she will allocate the time and deal with these items with her full attention.

An email like the one Homer received from his Line Foreman must be responded to immediately. In a similar instance, Louise would take the same course of action as Homer, but the difference is that she is always aware of where she needs to apply herself, even when new urgent requests cross her desk. In fact, the

Projecteze system has almost eliminated crisis situations from her day. She has moved from being reactive to proactive.

In her Projecteze Table, Louise captured all of the items she must act on and their timing. She doesn't have to try to remember them all; so she quickly gets on with her day. Since Louise began using the Projecteze method, whenever she interacts with another person, she is able to converse with a clear mind. She's fully present for them, fully in the moment to hear what they are saying. She knows that her level of communication has improved substantially since she started using Projecteze, and this gives her not only a great deal of satisfaction but also some inner peace. Her past tendency to react abruptly and with frustration when someone interrupted her has vanished. She found a method that frees her from stress and mental clutter. She's more available for all areas of her life.

This fictional tale of two people working in the same environment illustrates two very different experiences. One person is stressed and constantly being overwhelmed. The other is busy but under control. When Louise goes home at the end of the day, she leaves her work at work because it's all captured in her Projecteze Table. Homer, on the other hand, takes his mental "To Do List" home with him and recites it to himself, involuntarily, every couple of hours—throughout the night. Louise gets a much better sleep and is much more energized for work the next day. Homer always looks exhausted, because in spite of giving himself a weekend to recover from the office stress, he's continually worried about his job performance, as he mentally tries to sort through the jumble of information he knows is just waiting for him Monday morning.

Reduced stress, increased personal satisfaction and high personal productivity are usually associated with a sense of having some form of control over our situation. Projecteze provides you with a way to seize opportunities, relax more, be creative, and apply yourself with greater efficiency and effectiveness. It provides the means to free yourself from unnecessary stress and be more available for interaction and relationship building with others.

Most people relate to Homer's situation but would much rather experience the type of day Louise has. Without a method and a means to organize their workday, many people simply react and allow daily events to control them, which robs them of time, efficiency, effectiveness, and energy. "Where did the day go!" they often think. And for that matter, they might well ask, "Where did the week...the month...or even the year go?"

How can you use the Projecteze system in your work life? The second half of this chapter contains three examples of Projecteze Tables to illustrate how you can structure information packets and what you can expect from your Projecteze Table once you have put it into practice. First, I begin with an example from construction that shows how to coordinate many concurrent projects and contractors. The second example illustrates a single project that requires the coordination of several disciplines. And the third example is pertinent to consultants who have several projects and many clients.

The chapter concludes with some suggestions about how your Projecteze Table can help you to enjoy worry-free vacations —or any extended periods away from your office—because picking up where you left off when you return is a breeze with Projecteze.

## Commercial Construction:
## Many concurrent projects and contractors

The first example is one of my own Projecteze Tables, taken in early June a few years ago. It describes twelve completely different projects that I was overseeing and responsible for managing at the time.

One of these projects was a $5.7 million expansion to an existing facility that had to be kept open and fully operational throughout construction (see the top row in the table below with the project name "Central Facility Building Expansion"). What you see in this row are the commitments and action items I was tracking and monitoring. I was the owner's representative on this project which took twelve months to go from initial planning to completion. Not only did this multi-million dollar project come in ahead of schedule and 10% under budget, but I was focused and relatively stress-free throughout the entire process.

At first glance, you will see how long my entire Projecteze Table was and the level of detail it was able to absorb. This is typical. I've included it in its entirety so that you can see a realistic example of a Projecteze Table and get a sense of it as a living document. While this table covered over two months of scheduled action items, the most immediate ones that needed my attention during the first two weeks of June appear at the top of the table—front and center to my focus.

The items that are not preceded by a date describe tasks that needed to happen within a general timeframe but not on or by a specific date, as well as other reference information I wanted to have easy access to. In a few of the rows, I inserted key dates right from the project schedule. At a glance every morning, I could easily stay on top of these concurrent projects which involved many different contractors.

| Project | Date | Prty | Commitments & Action Items |
|---|---|---|---|
| **Central Facility Building Expansion** | Jun 8 | 1 | • June 7: Bruce to send sets of Final Development Permit dwgs (June 5 mtg)<br>• Discuss required intersection changes with Bill<br>• Bruce to confirm what the extra design fees will be for the mechanical redesign (May 30 mtg)<br>• Ask Joel how he wants us to deal with Security for the large number of construction personnel on-site<br>• June 9: Confirm with Al that the old building on the site is empty and ready for demolition.<br>• Fred to respond re: preparing PO for the Consultant; fees & disbursements to be included (June 7 email)<br>• Bruce & Laurence to get together to write Special Conditions and General Conditions (May 21)<br>• June 17 - 28: Old building demolition (per timing in May 27 email to Al)<br>• June 17: RFQ submissions from contractors due to Chris by this afternoon<br>• June 25: Mtg at MB to score pre-qualification submissions (May 24 email)<br>• July 8: Mtg with Dept Mgrs to go through drawings & finalize design<br>• July 18: Law Dept to send me comments on contract (per my June 3 email)<br>• July 19: Bruce to send me sets of completed dwgs & specs (3 x 11"x17", 2 x full size)<br>• July 25: Tender to go out to short-listed contractors; Chris to notify them where to get bid packages.<br>• Get separate quote for overhead doors; this will be dealt with as a Prime Cost Sum under the General Contractor agreement (May 22 mtg with Chris)<br>• Aug 8, 9:00 am: Pre-bid site tour for contractors<br>• Aug 16: Tender closing for construction contract<br>• Schedule Project Start-Up mtg with contractor awarded the project<br>• Aug: Bruce to send me a proposal for design/construction of the 32 Ave intersection revision; use to apply for funding next year (June 7) |
| **Northwest Light Rail Station Construction Close-out** | Jun 8 | 2 | • Email sent to Jim asking if he could get Tim to help us with the low lighting issue (May 10) Jim to discuss at breakfast meeting on June 7 (June 3)<br>• June 11: Phil asked to get two lights fixed—one on platform & new one in washroom (May 13; responded May 14 & will talk to Mark when he returns May 19). Phil is still pursuing (May 20). Email from Mark saying Concept will check it out by June 10 (May 29)<br>• June 11: Schedule follow-up of substantial completion inspection - for remaining (seasonal) items to be checked (March 25)<br>• June 15: Nick is still working on some of the record dwgs. Call Gordon approx May 4 to see where he is with these. (April 26). Gordon has the mechanical as-built drawings from Nick but not the electrical yet. He will send Nick an email asking where they are & when we can do another follow up inspection of the station. I told Gordon I would call him back in 2 weeks. (May 11). Phil has all of the drawings. I asked him to get them to me ASAP—CD + 3 sets of 11" x 17" hard copy (May 26). Email sent to Tim asking him to follow up on this (June 6) |

| Project | Date | Prty | Commitments & Action Items |
|---|---|---|---|
| **Facilities Drawings Database** | Jun 8 | 2 | • New database software program test failed. Being followed up to figure out why it wasn't working. Email sent to Mike asking if he could do a trial run with Joyce since he managed to get it working for him (May 7) See also follow-up email from Hank (May 19)<br>• Joyce to: (May 7)<br>1) Continue converting other dwgs and setting up indexes: approx 2 to 3 months;<br>2) Convert all AutoCAD dwgs to tiff & pdf;<br>3) Finish the indexing.<br>• Approx July 10: Joyce & I to get together to decide how to organize and password protect all of the indexes; and confirm how to add dwgs in the future. |
| **Parking Lots Development** | Jun 9 | 1 | • June 15: Brent to have defined a solution for the light poles (June 1)<br>CONSTRUCTION SCHEDULE:<br>• June 9 - 16: Excavation and removal<br>• June 15 – 20: Electrical<br>• June 19: Catch basins, leads & hydrants<br>• June 21 – 26: Concrete curbs<br>• June 23: SITE MTG (Facilities Boardroom)<br>• June 26 – 28: Gravel put down<br>• June 29 & 30: Paving<br>• June 30: SITE MTG (Facilities Boardroom)<br>• July 1 & 2: Line painting<br>• July 1–10: Landscaping<br>• July 11: Substantial Completion Inspection.<br>• July 18: Collect Contractor Security ID cards (5) from Mario |
| **Admin Building Renovation (minor)** | Jun 9 | 2 | • June 8: Mechanical Consultant to provide solution for maintaining space comfort during the reno, especially air conditioning (May 25 mtg)<br>• June 25: Architect to have floor plan converted into CADD (May 19) |
| **Indoor Air Quality Testing** | Jun 9 | 3 | • Talk to the Green Team re: what the major driver for the air testing request is<br>• Find out which local consultants can do the testing for us; ask Dick for suggestions<br>• Send out an RFP for proposals to at least three testing companies |
| **Fiscal Budget** | Jun 12 | 1 | • Prepare next fiscal budget and backup; must be done by June 30. Talk to Bryan, etc for scope and costing estimates on his projects targeted for next year.<br>• Review and update documents to be used for project budgeting back-up<br>• June 28: Submit budget to Jim |

| Project | Date | Prty | Commitments & Action Items |
|---|---|---|---|
| **Light Rail Station Platforms Restoration** | Jun 13 | 2 | • Set up a mtg with the Contractor for Bryan & I to get an understanding of why the tiles installation price was so high this year (see my email of April 20 to Bryan)<br>SCHEDULE: (May 3)<br>• June 3 – July 28: Station 25 renovation [UNDERWAY]<br>• June 28 – July 20: Station 14 renovation<br>• July 1 – 30: Stations 11 & 12 tiles installation<br>• July 4 & Aug 3 long weekends – tiles installation at Station 2<br>• July 9 – 18: CALGARY STAMPEDE (no work to be done on any platforms)<br>• July 15: Are the Station 7 warranty repairs finished??<br>• July 19 – Aug 7: NE Leg platforms sealed<br>• July 19 – Sept 13: Miscellaneous repairs at all stations<br>• Jacob to collect keys and security passes from General Contractor at the end of construction |
| **Heavy Equipment Replacement** | Jun 14 | 1 | • Week of June 14: Scott & John to visit, review and provide direction on the bay 14 unit. We need direction on this ASAP because no one seems to know where the slack is coming from in the SE leg that is causing problems with setting the legs. Unit could become unusable at any time. (May 10, May 14; May 21)<br>• June 14: Brad to a send list of names of other clients who have the same units in a similar environment (May 10, May 14). Scott is bringing this list with him on his trip (May 21)<br>• After week of June 14 mtg: Brad to confirm cost of the piston & cylinder assemblies. They must be replaced if the units need anything more than a seal kit (May 25)<br>• June 17: Brad to re-quote two sets of cover plates for AG after he talks to his head office on June 14 (June 3)<br>• July 16: Harold & Doug to make adaptations to units on T&M after units 5 & 6 are completed – approx mid July (OK'd by Jim; May 28)<br>• Did Harold finish fixing up the Foreman's Office wall? (May 10)<br>SCHEDULE:<br>• May 1 – July 7: Units 5 & 6 replaced<br>• June 23 - Sept 10: Units 11 & 12 replaced (major excavations) |
| **South Light Rail Stations Construction Turnovers**<br><br>South 1 (Stn 35)<br>South 2 (Stn 36) | Jun 18 | 2 | • June 18: Turnover of South 1 (Stn 35) platform and utility complex including railway pedestrian crossing<br>• June 21: Turnover of South 2 (Stn 36) platform and utility complex including railway pedestrian crossing<br>• June 21: CCTV Site Inspection and Central Security Image Review<br>• June 26: Turnover of track works, civil works, and landscaping within the track right of way<br>• June 26: Turnover of Traction Power, Signals, and C ommunications network.<br>• Jul 22: Turnover of South 1 parking lots and grounds including landscaping around the utility complex.<br>• July 22: Turnover of South 2 parking lots and grounds. |
| **Central Facility Electrical Upgrade** | Jun 24 | 1 | • June 23: Funding request for study was submitted for June 23 budget mtg (May 31)<br>• June 24: Send email to Consultant to confirm whether or not the budget has been approved and if we are "go" for the study<br>• Mid-August: Report due from Consultant for next year's Fiscal Capital Projects Budget request justification |

| Project | Date | Prty | Commitments & Action Items |
|---|---|---|---|
| **Remote Kiosks Construction** | Jul 5 | 2 | • July 4: Neil to confirm revised drawings of proposed facilities are acceptable. Then Consultant will issue for construction. (June 19 mtg)<br>• July 7: Tour all sites with Operations to confirm they are ready for construction to proceed.<br>• July 12: Randy to process PO requisition for General Contractor.<br>• July 15: Randy has awarded Fencing contract for all sites (fencing ready by July 6 for installation July 15 - 31). Randy to notify Contractor that the Site 3 installation is to be delayed into August. (June 28 mtg)<br>• July & Aug: Sites to be graded, concrete pads poured and buildings erected, for completion by Aug 30.<br>• End of July: Site 3 is on hold for now until after the land use agreement is signed. Neil to have received sign-off of the land use agreement with the adjacent land owner by the end of July. Neil to advise all when this has been completed (June 25 mtg)<br>• August: Additional signage to be installed; Neil to coordinate.<br>• Sept 5: Opening of new kiosks at all sites |
| **Vacation** | Aug 20 | 1 | • Set "Out of Office Asst" on & change voice mail recording |

## Oil and Gas Engineering:
## One major project involving many disciplines

The following example illustrates what you could expect a Projecteze Table to look like for a Project Manager overseeing the engineering design of a large oil and gas plant—a multi-billion dollar facility. This example represents a project that engaged a team of 85 people in 13 disciplines. Scope and timing for this design project was captured on a 7,000-line project schedule covering a two-year time frame.

For this type of project, the Project Manager's most immediate attention is focused on the objectives (deliverables) that are coming due over the next several weeks and months. The following Projecteze Table was created by the Project Manager transferring items from the project schedule that had milestone dates between Oct 14th (the current date) and Nov 30th (six weeks ahead). In this table, each engineering discipline got its own row. High-level tasks were entered by discipline, as they appeared in the project schedule. In this way, it was an easy process to transfer milestones straight from the schedule and into a Projecteze Table. By focusing on the milestone dates of the key deliverables for each discipline, the Project Manager is better able to coordinate everyone across the project and keep it on track.

After populating the "Commitments & Action Items" with high-level objectives from the project schedule, the Project Manager assigned a priority and next action date (in the Date column) for each row (discipline). The date and priority assigned to each row pertained to the next action item in that row. Then the table was sorted by *Date - Prty*.

This Projecteze Table provides the Project Manager with a tool for tracking each deliverable as its deadline date approaches. By tracking each item as it bubbles to the top of the table, the Project Manager is able to speak with the appropriate Discipline Leads about their next deliverable and track its status. With this approach, the Project Manager will know immediately when something is going to be late, what the delay is going to be, and what impact it will have on other dependent deliverables. The Project Manager will know what they need to know as early as possible. In a non-confrontational way, the Project Manager will also continually reinforce to the team the importance of meeting deadlines and sticking to the schedule. They will definitely be on top of everything. Coordinating projects using the Projecteze method strengthens communications and increases efficiency.

| Project | Date | Prty | Commitments & Action Items |
|---------|------|------|----------------------------|
| **Earthworks** | Oct 15 | 3 | • Oct 15: Filter/manipulate Lidar data<br>• Oct 26: PDA drawing |
| **Mechanical** | Oct 16 | 2 | • Oct 16: Mech equip list IFR—Plant, Pads & PLs<br>• Oct 17: Long lead delivery items MRQ list<br>• Nov 16: Mech equip list IFA—Plant |
| **Piping** | Oct 17 | 1 | • Oct 17: Pads Plot Plan IFR<br>• Oct 24: Equipment layout IFR, WBS Area Key Plan IFR<br>• Oct 26: WBS Area Key Plan IFA<br>• Oct 29: Plant Plot Plan IFA<br>• Nov 13: 3D piping model development—Plant<br>• Nov 23: Equipment layout IFA, Material lists for valves, pipe & fittings, welds (MTO)-Plant |

| Project | Date | Prty | Commitments & Action Items |
|---|---|---|---|
| Process | Oct 19 | 1 | • Oct 19: P&IDs Pads & PLs – issue IFR<br>• Nov 1: Major Equip DS to Mech<br>• Nov 9: PFDs, MB & P&IDs Plant - issue IFA |
| Instrumentation | Oct 19 | 2 | • Oct 19: EI&C P&ID input (tagging & logic)<br>• Nov 2: Prelim Instrument index (for est. only) IFA<br>• Nov 9: Controls Input to Electrical UPS sizing<br>• Nov 30: Priced instrument MTO |
| Pipelines | Oct 19 | 2 | • Oct 19: PL plans and routing<br>• Oct 26: Preliminary PL ROW crossing designs (IFR)<br>• Nov 2: PL requirements (Pigging, heat tracing, materials), PL Loop Designs (IFR)<br>• Nov 5: PL development plan (IFR)<br>• Nov 9: PL 3D modeling<br>• Nov 14: PL alignment sheets (IFR)<br>• Nov 23: PL profile drawings (IFR), PL GA Drawings, PL stress analysis<br>• Nov 29: PL MTOs |
| Contracts | Oct 20 | 3 | • Oct 20: Contracts Strategy (IFR) |
| Electrical | Oct 26 | 2 | • Oct 26: 3D Modeling Elec Tray—Plant<br>• Oct 30: Elec. Plot / Key Plans<br>• Oct 31: Revise elec installation details, Coordination of Overall SLDs<br>• Nov 9: Calculations—Construction Power Loads<br>• Nov 23: Prelim Elec MCC building layouts (changes) IFR |
| Controls | Oct 26 | 2 | • Oct 26: Control System Architecture Dwg IFR |
| Project Engineering | Oct 30 | 1 | • Oct 30: Work Breakdown Structure<br>• Nov 30: Design Basis Memorandum |
| Civil /Structural | Nov 1 | 3 | • Nov 1: Bldg budget quotes<br>• Nov 23: Prelim plant structural |
| Project Services | Nov 5 | 3 | • Nov 5: Class 4 Estimate compiled |
| Procurement | Nov 6 | 3 | • Nov 6: Long lead bidders list |

Creating a Projecteze Table from a project schedule can be done quickly and easily, making critical information much more accessible for the Project Manager. I've used an example from the oil and gas industry, but you can easily imagine this structure being applied to any project that requires a high degree of coordination among people from different disciplines working on the same project. For example, I could see this kind of table being used by an artistic director scheduling a season of plays; a marina operator keeping track of maintenance, scheduling, storage, and accounting activities; a college dean organizing a major international conference; or a community organizer over-seeing the establishment of a new health center.

The Projecteze system enables anyone to be proactive and stay on top of details that originate from many contributors—and that keeps the entire project team focused and on track with everyone moving in the same direction. The Projecteze Table supports and enables essential communication, while reinforcing accountability by all team members.

### Consulting: Many clients, each with several projects

The following Projecteze Table illustrates how an independent marketing consultant using a Projecteze Table can easily track several projects across a variety of clients, while she is also taking care of managing and growing her own business—Hoola Hoop Marketing. This consultant has more than one project on the go for some of her clients. You will see that this Projecteze Table contains five columns, one being added for "Client".

When the consultant speaks to any one of those clients on the phone, she can re-sort her Projecteze Table immediately by *Client*, *Date* and *Prty*, in the way the table below is sorted. This will organize the rows by client in order of her next pressing commitment or action item. See the rows for Do-Wop Developers in the table below.

This enables the consultant to quickly identify everything she has committed to for that specific client or is waiting for that client to deliver, in order of date and priority. Discussing these items quickly and efficiently leaves the client with the impression that the consultant is really on top of her game—which she is!

After discussing what needs to be covered with her client, our consultant can immediately re-sort her table by *Date* and *Prty* to give her an awareness of all issues confronting her for that day and their relative priority across all of her clients.

| Client | Project | Date | Prty | Commitments & Action Items |
|---|---|---|---|---|
| **Centre For Lunar Reclamation** | Develop Plan | Jan 31 | 1 | • Jan 31: Prepare Invoice<br>• Marketing Plan developed with budget<br>• Sales Plan developed for March Event<br>• Key words and network mapping<br>• Get internal lists together |
| **Dontcha Trust** | Sales Lead Generation | Jan 27 | 1 | • Jan 27: Review copy from Cheryl and John. Re-draft landing page copy<br>• Jan 28: Schedule a follow-up call<br>• Feb 10: Update Wireframes |
| **Do-Wop Developers** | Housing Campaign | Jan 26 | 1 | • Jan 26: PPC Campaign edits due from client<br>• Jan 26: Analyze traffic flow patterns<br>• Jan 31: Develop Exec Summary – Strategic Plan<br>• Jan 31: SEO updates to site |
| **Do-Wop Developers** | Marketing Coaching | Feb 10 | 1 | • Call Keith for background docs.<br>• Feb: Research and develop strategic and creative briefs |
| **Do-Wop Developers** | Lead Management | Feb 10 | 3 | • Waiting to hear back on timeline (Jan 20 tel call) |
| **Foggy Meaning** | Being Profitable™ | Feb 15 | 1 | • Feb 15: Set follow-up meeting (Jan 21 mtg) |
| **Hoola Hoop Marketing** | Accounting | Jan 26 | 2 | • Get Employee / Internet Access Codes to Lyla – Carol to find<br>• Get the Dec / Jan 15 Emp. Remittance Form – Carol (to Lyla)<br>• Jan 27 - Finalize Invoices<br>• Feb 28 - Big Line<br>• Feb 28 - Get procedures manual prepared – Carol |
| **Hoola Hoop Marketing** | Being Profitable™ | Jan 27 | 1 | • Jan 27: Confirm Pen Box order<br>• Feb 15: Complete quotes list - Kathy<br>• Feb 28: Finish edits to all chapters; 2 days – 6 at a time<br>• Feb 28: Edits 3rd Party – internal<br>• Mar 15: Edits to be done by professional editor<br>• April 15: Get Copy to Carey to flow into design<br>• Prepare Section 3 purpose |
| **Hoola Hoop Marketing** | Infrastructure | Feb 15 | 1 | • Feb 15: Purchase Master Suite upgrade - CDR Quoted<br>• Fix accounting system – clean up computer<br>• Add DVD drive into contractor station<br>• PC fix software purchase<br>• Get better backup device<br>• Get lighting setup for video |

| Client | Project | Date | Prty | Commitments & Action Items |
|---|---|---|---|---|
| **Hoola Hoop Marketing** | Research | Feb 15 | 3 | • Feb 15: Finish Competitive Analysis<br>• Investigate small business financing<br>• Investigate video / lighting training<br>• Research local wireless digital security services<br>• Read book – "Do You Care" and comments on webpage |
| **Hoola Hoop Marketing** | Human Capital Development | Feb 28 | 3 | • Job Descriptions<br>• Job Ads & Web copy<br>• Develop procedures manuals<br>• Web upload resume form |
| **Leave Me Alone Expeditions** | Lead Generation | Jan 27 | 1 | • Jan 27: Check-up on PPC campaign<br>• Jan 28: Follow-up with Jane (Jan 16 mtg) |
| **Mental Heritage** | General | Jan 26 | 1 | • Jan 26: Process Credit Card Orders (send emails to Jared)<br>• Jan 26: Cross ref business cards<br>• Jan 26: Follow-up on all the leads ASAP<br>• Jan 26: Call Jared to coordinate training<br>• Jan 28: Integration (Kathy)<br>• Feb 08: Edit Plan for marketing group<br>• Feb 15: Develop draft job descriptions for James (see budget for titles) |
| Personal | House | Feb 5 | 2 | • Feb 5: Get three quotes for new roof<br>• Feb 10: Get spare room ready for visitors |
| Personal | Fitness | Feb 15 | 2 | • Read Grant's Book |
| **Smoke Signal Pasta** | Website & Marketing | Jan 31 | 2 | • Follow-up with Dave re: proposal – Jim to call |
| **Squadron Leaflets** | Being Profitable™ & Marketing Design Projects | Jan 25 | 1 | • Set up distribution account; must integrate with payment system<br>• Set up payment account<br>• Set up shipping accounts<br>• Define site security solution<br>• Work with Kathy on website design: site map, wire frame, use cases, systems architecture<br>• Structure the PR copy first; finish it and the website copy together (Dec 19 mtg)<br>• Update the Marketing Plan |

**Vacations and Other Absences:**
**Taking the stress out of leaving work and returning**

*No man needs a vacation so much*
*as the man who has just had one.*
—Elbert Hubbard

Have you ever had the experience of taking a vacation and feeling anxious about being absent from your post or even more anxious about what you will find when you return to work? That first day back from vacation can be traumatic for many people, but with the Projecteze system, you will literally ease back into work mode, knowing that you will quickly be able to manage all the new information that has arrived in your absence. Here's an illustration of the process I use to get on top of my work after a vacation or even after a work-related absence such as a conference or training course.

Let's say you've scheduled a two-week vacation and it starts tomorrow. If you don't have anyone to fill in for you, your Projecteze Table will be a wonderful reminder of where your work needs to resume when you return. On that first day back, the first thing you will do is take a quick look at your Projecteze Table and identify the key issues you noted prior to going away. You will quickly recall all the commitments and action items that are the most pressing.

Next you will start going through your email inbox, which is likely to be quite full and contain new information about your projects. As you read through each email, capture all the pertinent bits of information about any new commitments and action items that impact you and paste them into your Projecteze Table. After you do this, file each email into sub-folders pre-named by project or correspondent. That gets them out of your inbox and out of your way; you will handle every piece of email only once. After you finish going through your email, the main window of your email inbox should be empty. What a great feeling!

Laurence Seton © | Projecteze Inc.

I use this technique every day. I read an email. Ask myself, "Does it have anything in it that will impact me?" If it does, I capture the pertinent details in my Projecteze Table and then file all email into sub-folders. Presto! My inbox is empty again.

Initially, getting into this habit requires some effort and focus, but as you practice it will become second nature to you. By using this method, both my desk and email inbox are clean, and I am ready to respond with a clear mind as new challenges or unexpected surprises arise. In the meantime, I am positioned as best as I can be to deal with the priorities I have already identified and am working on.

Let's return to our example. After having gone through all your email and transferred the pertinent information into your Projecteze Table, go through the table and reorganize the information. As you do this, ask yourself:

1) Does each new information packet have an action flag date?

2) Are the information packets arranged in the Commitments & Action Items column of each row by the level of urgency and next action date?

3) Do the dates in my Date column and priorities in my Prty column correspond to the next item in my Commitments & Action Items column for each row?

Then re-sort your table by *Date* and *Prty*. As you know, your highest priority commitments and action items will be sitting at the top of your Projecteze Table. On your first day back after two weeks away, you will be organized very quickly. This whole process usually takes less than one or two hours to complete, and you'll feel the satisfaction of knowing that you are once again on top of everything. Your stress level remains low because you know right away where to direct your focus and apply your energy.

Hypothetically, let's extend our example and consider the situation when you are away from the office and in your absence someone else will fill in for you to keep your projects moving forward.

In this case, ensure your Projecteze Table is completely up to date on the afternoon of the last day before you leave. Save a copy of that table under a new name, remove any confidential or personal information and remove the password protection; trim it down to just what you want others to see. Then print off two copies of this abbreviated version of your Projecteze Table and sit down with the person who is going to be filling in for you and review it together. Explain the issues and answer any questions they may have. Your abbreviated Projecteze Table will tell the other person exactly what is coming up and when, as well as where reference documents are stored—because it will all be described in your table. Then email your abbreviated Projecteze Table to that person before you leave. Again, make sure you have removed the password protection.

If the person filling in for you is familiar with the Projecteze system, he or she can even manage and update your table for you while you are away. When you come back, they can email you the up-to-date version of your table so that as soon as you walk in the door, you will know exactly what is coming at you based on actions that person took in your absence. With a simple *copy-paste* process, you can recombine the updated information from the abbreviated table into your personal and confidential original within a matter of minutes, fully restoring your complete Projecteze Table with current information on all your projects. You can be up and running as soon as you return.

At the beginning of this chapter I gave you an example of two workers. Homer was continually dealing with "the pain of it all"—losing focus, effectiveness, and sleep. Louise, by using the Projecteze system, was current in all her work-related responsibilities, more relaxed, confident and efficient no matter what the day brought.

Like Louise, Homer could have chosen to build and organize a simple Projecteze Table that would sort his priorities in a variety of ways: by concurrent projects, by disciplines within a project, or by client for multiple projects across several clients.

When it came time to take a vacation or to be absent from the office for a week or two, you can guess, thinking about our fictional characters, which one was able not only to find greater enjoyment while away, but return refreshed and ready to leap back into the workday with renewed efficiency and enthusiasm.

# V

## Self-Discipline And
## Keeping Your Projecteze Table Alive

*The whole secret of freedom from anxiety
over not having enough time
lies not in working more hours,
but in the proper planning of the hours.*
—Anonymous

Your Projecteze Table will work well if you use it regularly and diligently. You get out of it what you put in to it. Incorporate Projecteze into your workday and it will serve you extremely well.

Using Projecteze on a daily basis does require self-discipline and dedication. But by routinely performing just a few basic steps every day, you will quickly benefit from the power of Projecteze. If you are not a systematic person by nature–and yet you still want to be more organized–then resolve to teach yourself this small discipline. Making Projecteze a habit will pay huge dividends because you will continually reinforce the basic techniques for achieving excellence all on your projects.

How long will it take you to acquire this element of self-discipline? I encourage you to commit to setting up your own Projecteze Table and using it daily for at least one month. This adjustment period will usually be enough for you to acquire the habit and fully realize the benefits Projecteze offers.

This chapter describes a daily routine I recommend for working with your Projecteze Table. The first part offers some observations and suggestions about processing electronic information for capture into your Projecteze Table and how to go about it. The second part of the chapter outlines a daily routine that keeps your Projecteze Table a living document working for you. At the end of this chapter is a flow chart that illustrates the daily Projecteze routine.

**Processing Electronic Information**

*Knowing a great deal is not the same as being smart;*
*intelligence is not information alone but also judgment,*
*the manner in which information is collected and used.*
–Dr. Carl Sagan

When you're working at your computer–processing documents, tables, or emails–the *Edit>Copy>Paste* functions work very well for capturing information straight from original electronic documents and placing it into your Projecteze Table. You can also *copy-paste* links to other documents on your network or websites that you will need for future reference. This makes it very quick and easy to get at frequently accessed resources.

With the large volume of email you receive, there is the risk of losing critical details and information in the ever-mounting pile in the inbox. Your Projecteze Table is the place to capture just the information you need as it comes to you. As I mentioned at the end of the previous chapter, here's a simple practice to incorporate into your daily email reading routine.

Have your Projecteze Table open on your computer desktop. As you sort through your email, *copy-paste* into your table only the essential portions of current correspondence that describe commitments and action items that impact you. As you do this, move each email out of your inbox and into a specific email sub-folder. Adding a note at the end of an information packet in your Projecteze Table describing that the item came from an email, who it came from, and the date you received it makes it easy to track down the original at any time. Following these steps always provides me with a big sense of relief, because I find that an inbox with 5 or 10 emails in it is a lot less overwhelming than an inbox with thousands of emails in it. And what a great feeling it is to have cleared through all of the email and have a completely empty inbox. This tells me I have captured all the vital information and it is sitting in one, centralized location–my Projecteze Table.

Here's another technique for transferring electronic information into your table from other sources. As you *copy-paste* data or text into your Projecteze Table, it will often have a different format (font type and size, etc.) than what you are using for your table. In order to keep your table looking good, there are two options that will enable you to easily deal with the formatting that might accompany pasted text.

The first and easiest technique is to paste copied text into your Projecteze Table as "Unformatted Text". After copying what you want to capture, place your cursor in your table where you want to paste it. Then select *Edit>Paste Special>Unformatted Text*. The text you paste will automatically take on the formatting that is already set up around it in your table. This is perhaps the easiest approach.

The second approach is to the use the *Format Painter* in MS Word (it is an icon that looks like a Paintbrush in your toolbar). You can use the *Format Painter* to transfer formatting you like and have previously set up in your Projecteze Table, and apply it to text you've transferred from another source. Highlight the text that has the formatting you want to copy. One click on the *Format Painter* icon will give you one application. Two clicks on the icon lets you continue to paint on formatting as much as you like. In a matter of seconds, you can have all of your new information looking just the way you want it. As I described in Chapter Two, I recommend 10 point Times New Roman with a hanging indent to provide a well organized, easy-to-read document.

By maintaining your Projecteze Table as a personal document, you will always be solely responsible for what it contains and to what degree it gets maintained. It is yours. This puts the responsibility for its content squarely on your shoulders alone.

To establish your table as a personal document, you can apply password protection to prevent others from opening and viewing it. You can always share any portion of the information contained within your table by using *copy-paste* onto a blank page. If your Projecteze Table contains confidential or personal information and you choose to print out your entire table, be careful where you leave it.

These are processes I've used successfully with the Projecteze system for many years.

# Daily Projecteze Routine

*Self-discipline is crucial to a simpler,*
*more contented life.*
—Tenzin Gyatso, the 14 th Dalai Lama

Breathing life into your Projecteze Table is what gives it the power to become the most practical and efficient organizational system you've ever used. Returning to your Projecteze Table on a daily basis is a critical aspect of this method. I find it usually takes ten or fifteen minutes, once or twice a day to keep my table up to date. This is time I recover many times over because of the efficiencies built into the system. When I describe your Projecteze Table as a living document, I mean that it is an inter-active tool that thrives when nourished by the discipline of your daily attention. It expands and contracts as you use it.

All of the steps in my Projecteze method have been simplified as much as possible. These steps will become habitual and intu-itive in a very short period of time. This, in turn, means you can quickly focus on the content of your Projecteze Table instead of having to spend valuable time managing a complex or rigid organizational system.

By following the daily routine I recommend, you will not only condition yourself to properly plan and execute your work but you will also reinforce strong organizational habits as you practise the discipline required to accomplish many things. I encourage you to adhere to this regimen with determination and resolve for at least one month. Stick with it and integrate the process into your day until it becomes instinctive.

Keep your Projecteze Table up to date. If you do, it will always be pertinent. I recommend that you follow these seven simple steps as part of your daily routine:

1) *At the beginning of your day,* open your Projecteze
   Table from the previous day and re-save it, only
   modifying the document name with the current date.

Always use two digits for the day (e.g. *LSeton-2009-04-25*).

2) *Review* your Projecteze Table and create a short list in your project notebook of critical commitments and action items showing up for you that day for easy reference, or print out a complete copy of your Projecteze Table to take with you to meetings. Often, there will be five to ten key issues I need to focus on in a day, before other issues start coming at me. Instead of printing out my entire Projecteze Table, I will list those action items on the next clean page in my notebook, along with when and where my meetings are. That one page is what I will follow for the day.

3) *In meetings and from interactions with others*, capture new commitments and action items that impact you in your notebook, as they come up.

4) *During the day and as you have time*, keep your Projecteze Table current. Transfer new key commitments and action items from your project notebook into your Projecteze Table during the day—from your meetings, telephone conversations, meeting minutes, email or project schedules. Do this during breaks between meetings or whenever you can get back to your desktop or laptop computer. As action items are completed, check them off in your notebook and delete them from your Projecteze Table.

5) *Re-sort your table* as frequently as you need to throughout the day. As you revise the next-action date in the Date column for a row, re-sort your table. This will move that row out of your way and let you focus on the remaining priorities for the day. This is especially helpful if your table shows more than one page full of projects (rows) for the current day.

6) *At the end of the day*, make sure you've entered all the new commitments and action items (that directly affect you) from that day. Add new rows for new projects and delete items in your table that were completed.

As you transfer items into your table, check them off in your project notebook to show they have either been dealt with or are captured in your Projecteze Table. This way you will never have to look back in your notebook. Your Projecteze Table will have it all and will be the only place you'll need to refer to.

- Whenever you can, have the follow-up date leading each information packet in the Commitments & Action Items column.

- Using *click* and *drag*, rearrange the information packets within the Commitments & Action Items column for each row so the next most immediate and highest priority issues are at the top *for each row.*

- Re-set the date in the Date column and priority in the Prty column according to the next most immediate action item showing up in the Commitments & Action Items column.

- Re-sort your table by *Date* and *Prty.* In a fraction of a second, this sort will bring all of the highest priority and next most immediate commitments and action items for the following day to the top of your table.

- Review your table and especially the rows that show up for the following day. This will remind you of what is coming up, starting first thing in the morning. At the end of my day, I will often prepare the page in my notebook for the following day with a list of key commitments, action items and meetings (from my calendar). This enables me to come in the following morning, grab my notebook and be up and active in a matter of seconds, knowing I'm on top of everything.

7) *Repeat daily.* At the end of every day, you'll be able to head out of the office and let it all go for the night, knowing that it's all captured, well organized and waiting for you in your Projecteze Table.

## Flowchart of Daily Projecteze Steps

The daily Projecteze routine is summarized in the following flow chart.

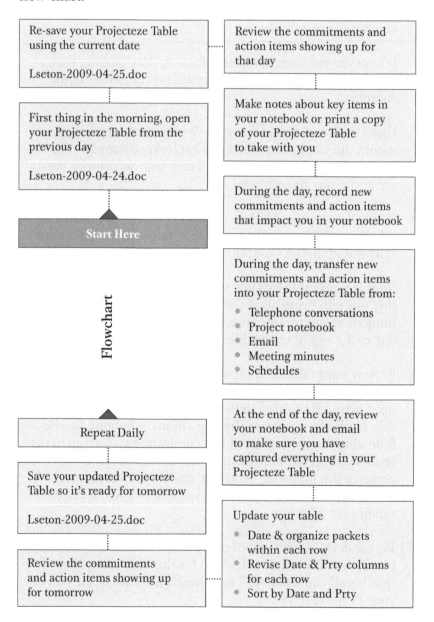

Laurence Seton © | Projecteze Inc.

As you continue to use the Projecteze system more and more, you will have a hard time doing without it. Every time you update your Projecteze Table for the next day you are setting yourself up for success. This one step helps you to mentally prepare for the following day.

You can walk out of your office with a clear mind knowing that everything you need to remember in order to be on top of all your projects is sitting there waiting for you. Gone are the sleepless nights of mentally reciting what you're supposed to be doing the next day. Thanks to Projecteze, you've already got those hours planned as efficiently as possible. And it's such a simple process.

When your work stays in the office and doesn't follow you home, the result is freedom—and that has lifestyle benefits. Away from the office, when you spend time with family and friends, you can be more fully present and available for them. After a peaceful night's rest free from mental clutter, you'll be able to head back into the office—energized and ready to start a new day with a fresh outlook.

# VI

## Building And Customizing
## Your Own Projecteze Table

*Simplicity is about subtracting the obvious
and adding the meaningful.*
–John Maeda

In the previous chapters, I showed you how to set up and use a Projecteze Table, and how to populate the rows and sort by columns. I also provided illustrations from my own experience. Now you should be ready to begin to use Projecteze for yourself. The first part of this chapter will help you set up your own table and the second part will describe ways to customize it to suit your own needs so that you too can be on top of everything.

## Building Your Own Projecteze Table

A great way to start is to use the table you set up in Chapter Two or you can download another blank template of the table from the website www.OnTopOfEverything.com.

If you are using the table you set up in Chapter Two, clear the data in all the rows below the header row. Highlight all of the information starting in the second row and down to the last cell in the bottom row. Hit the *Delete* key. This will clear the table of information and still leave the table intact with its formatting.

Name the document: *yourfirst initial lastname-yyyy-mm-dd*. You are now ready to start filling in your personal table with information from your own projects.

Expect to spend several hours populating your table the first time, with pertinent commitments and action items from all your projects. Gather everything you can think of that impacts you—from the stickies that cover your desk and computer, your *To Do* lists, notes from your project notebook, emails, schedules, and meeting minutes. As I mentioned in Chapter Three, keep your information packets simple, concise and to the point. Divide your work into logical categories (rows)—by project, by discipline, by client, or by process—whatever suits your sense of organization and your needs.

Capture all outstanding items that impact you and that require follow-up action by you or someone else—include them in your table. Resist the temptation to add general information describing aspects of your projects for which no follow-up action is required. Information of this type doesn't need to be tracked and can be stored elsewhere for reference, such as in project folders– one location for hard copy and one for electronic copy. If they are required for future reference, include a note in your Projecteze Table describing where you can find these materials and documents.

After populating your Projecteze Table for a few hours, watch it build and grow–all the while knowing that you are gaining control. Take pleasure in throwing out each sticky as you capture the action item from it. Check off descriptions in your notebook. Throw out *To Do* lists. Feel a deep sense of satisfaction as you capture data and notes from the myriad of other places you previously stored them. See the clutter clear as you transfer them into your one and only centralized Projecteze Table.

The key in the initial set up of your Projecteze Table is to stick with the process. Keep at it until everything is entered. Allow yourself several days to completely populate your first table. Once your table is assembled, ongoing management gets easier and faster as you master the simple sorting mechanisms. There's great satisfaction in deleting completed items and watching the next high priority items bubble to the top of your table.

After you use your own Projecteze Table for a week or two, quickly review the seven steps and flow chart at the end of Chapter Five to confirm you understand the steps to follow, why you're following them, and that you're comfortable with all of them. Enter this action item into your Projecteze Table now.

As you use your Projecteze Table daily, it will become more and more intuitive. Within a few weeks of employing this method, you will come to appreciate just how few steps there are to follow, how simple the system is, and how beneficial it is for staying on top of everything.

## Customizing Your Projecteze Table

The layout and formatting of the Projecteze Table that I've described is very effective. There are, however, situations when you might need to customize your table further. The Projecteze system is very flexible when it comes to customizing it for your own needs. A key flexibility with the Projecteze system is that you can choose which columns you will use to sort by.

You will recall that the basic Projecteze Table has four columns:

1) Project
2) Date
3) Prty
4) Commitments & Action Items

MS Word provides the ability to sort by any one or more of these columns individually or as a multiple column sort. You can, as I've suggested, sort by *Date* and *Prty* to arrange your Projecteze Table in order of projects by decreasing priority for each date.

Sorting by only the *Project* column can also be very helpful. In many cases, projects within an organization are assigned a project number (e.g. 2346-0809). By entering the project number as the first description in the Project column of each row, you will be able to sort by those project numbers.

The following example shows how you can add much more information to the columns you are sorting by and still retain the ability to sort by those columns. **MS Word will sort any column by the first line of information or leading description contained in each row of that column.**

*The rows in the following Projecteze Table were sorted by Date:*

| Project | Date | Prty | Commitments & Action Items |
|---------|------|------|----------------------------|
| 2346-0809<br>Client contact:<br>Brian Jones<br>786-9087 | Jan 17 | 1 | |
| 1256-5698<br>Client contact:<br>Blair Gibson<br>250-4569 | Jan 25 | 2 | |
| 9546-8523<br>Client contact:<br>Jason Stuart<br>561-8697 | Feb 10 | 2 | |
| 2589-1563<br>Client contact:<br>Pete Harris<br>769-0007 | Apr 5 | 2 | |
| 2346-0810<br>Client contact:<br>Susan Hilary<br>249-3481 | May 15 | 2 | |

*Re-sorting this table by the Project column provides you with a sequencing of projects by project number as shown here:*

| Project | Date | Prty | Commitments & Action Items |
|---------|------|------|----------------------------|
| 1256-5698<br>Client contact:<br>Blair Gibson<br>250-4569 | Jan 25 | 2 | |
| 2346-0809<br>Client contact:<br>Brian Jones<br>786-9087 | Jan 17 | 1 | |
| 2346-0810<br>Client contact:<br>Susan Hilary<br>249-3481 | May 15 | 2 | |
| 2589-1563<br>Client contact:<br>Pete Harris<br>769-0007 | Apr 5 | 2 | |
| 9546-8523<br>Client contact:<br>Jason Stuart<br>561-8697 | Feb 10 | 2 | |

The ability to enter additional information into any column and retain sort-ability makes this system infinitely customizable. You can use this feature to add information that you need to refer to often and that will not likely change during the course of a project. Key contacts and their telephone numbers, addresses or billing codes are examples of information you can place here. You could even insert another table into a column for a specific row, or for every row, to make data entry consistent and that much easier for each new project. This information will always be readily available for you at a glance. Here's an example:

| Project | Date | Prty | Commitments & Action Items | | |
|---------|------|------|----------------------------|---|---|
| 1256-5698 | Jan 25 | 2 | • Follow up with John on development permit application | | |
| | | | **Client Contacts** | **Telephone** | **Cell** |
| | | | Blair Gibson | 250-4569 | 812-1350 |
| | | | John Fillmore | 250-2598 | 258-2985 |
| | | | Jane Parker | 250-4516 | 236-1569 |

The process of inserting a table within a table is described in greater detail in Chapter Seven.

You might also benefit by adding another column to your Projecteze Table. Perhaps you have many projects assigned to you by several different clients, as we showed in our Hoola Hoop Marketing example in Chapter Four. You could add a column into your table and name it "Client". This will reduce the width of your Commitments & Action Items column, but adding that extra column may be so valuable that it will be well worth it. Sorting by *Client* enables you to quickly scan all of the pending and outstanding commitments to and from a specific client in very little time, by priority or by date. This provides you with easy reference points during your telephone calls and discussions with each client. You will not only sound like you're on top of your work, you will be!

I've added a column labeled *Client* to the following table and then sorted by *Client* and *Date*. The most timely commitments and action items that need to be discussed with each client will be grouped for easy reference. Make notes during your conversation with the client and then transfer those updates right into your Projecteze Table at your earliest convenience.

| Project | Client | Date | Prty | Commitments & Action Items |
|---|---|---|---|---|
| 1256-5698<br>Client contact:<br>Blair Gibson<br>250-4569 | ABC | Jan 25 | 2 | |
| 2346-0810<br>Client contact:<br>Susan Hilary<br>249-3481 | ABC | May 15 | 1 | |
| 9546-8523<br>Client contact:<br>Jason Stuart<br>561-8697 | ABC | Jun 15 | 2 | |
| 2346-0809<br>Client contact:<br>Brian Jones<br>786-9087 | XYZ | Jan 17 | 1 | |
| 2589-1563<br>Client contact:<br>Pete Harris<br>769-0007 | XYZ | Apr 5 | 2 | |

As you add columns to your Projecteze Table, the Commitments & Action Items column will, by default, become narrower. This is a very important column because it holds most of your information.

I must caution you against adding too many columns to your table. The recommended structure of the Projecteze Table is for only *four* columns—for good reason. After much of trial and error, I have found that keeping the table to four columns maintains the simplicity that is such a valuable aspect of the Projecteze system.

I recommend that you don't add any columns to your table beyond the four basic ones unless there is a very real benefit for you to have more. If you do add another column, and in order to retain a good width for the Commitments & Action Items column, you could change your page setup from portrait orientation to landscape orientation. This will give you an additional two and a half inches in width for this column.

As a manager, you might justify adding an "Employee" or "Team Member" column or a "By" column to your Projecteze Table. This could result in many rows for each project but could be very useful for grouping tasks by team member. To keep this column narrow, use a short heading and use only staff or team members' initials for their row. A quick re-sort by this column will quickly give you a grouping of the sub-projects or specific tasks each staff member is working on.

Your Projecteze Table can be a very powerful tool for staff reviews and for monitoring their progress. Be aware that a tool this powerful can also be misused to micro-manage employees. No one wants to experience the feeling of being manipulated that usually goes along with being micro-managed. Employed properly, however, your Projecteze Table can actually enhance team cohesiveness.

In the interest of fostering a team-oriented environment, I encourage you to use the techniques I described earlier. *Ask* your employees or team members what dates they can have their tasks completed by, and if the dates are okay with you, accept them. Then use your Projecteze Table to record those dates along with when those commitments were made, and to track your employees' progress.

Hold each person in your group accountable for the objectives and dates they have committed to. Focus on the status of macro-tasks rather than the many micro-steps required to complete each task. Focus on the satisfactory completion of each objective and not so much on what individual steps were taken to reach completion. Evaluate the finished product. By doing this, you will be exhibiting your faith in your team, and in all likelihood, they will find your management style, guided by your Projecteze Table, very motivating. Your team will appreciate your professional approach and will quickly come to realize you are on top of your projects and are counting on them to fulfill their commitments.

If you decide to hold project reviews as a group, try printing just the pertinent portion of your Projecteze Table (you can use *copy-paste* to place that portion onto a clean page) to create a handout for your meeting. Everyone will see exactly what each person has committed to and what you are tracking. Presenting information in this way helps to foster accountability with everyone. Quite literally, everyone will be working off the same page.

At the end of the meeting, everyone should be able to leave knowing exactly what each person is doing and what the objectives are for the week. Then, as soon as possible, update your Projecteze Table with the latest information arising from the meeting. Both the people you work with and your clients will appreciate how consistently reliable you are. Beyond this, there are more suggestions on how to set up and use a Team Projecteze Table in Chapter Ten.

You are probably starting to understand just how useful the Projecteze system can be and how simple–yet customizable–it is for meeting your own specific needs. One of the greatest benefits associated with customizing your Projecteze Table will be the efficiency and effectiveness you will achieve in your work.

There is no limit to the adaptability of Projecteze. I encourage you to share ideas on how you have customized your Projecteze Table and the benefits you have gained. Tell us where and how you are using the Projecteze system to improve your own efficiency and effectiveness. Share your "Aha!" experiences with everyone else at the website www.OnTopOfEverything.com. By compiling the experiences and successes we each have with Projecteze, we can all benefit.

# VII

## Becoming Proficient With Projecteze

*Anticipate the difficult by managing the easy.*
−Lao Tzu

As you become more experienced using Projecteze, you will benefit from applying additional dimensions to your tables. In this chapter, I offer 14 tips and practical techniques you can use to enhance your use of Projecteze.

1) **Meetings and Agendas Made Easy.** If you are going to a specific meeting and need to go over a series of points from your Projecteze Table with someone else or a group, simply *copy-paste* the pertinent information from the Commitments & Action Items column for that project onto a new sheet and print it out—all within a matter of seconds.

   If you have one or a series of back-to-back meetings for projects that are described in your Projecteze Table, simply print off your entire table and take it with you. You'll walk into every one of those meetings prepared—with notes about your key commitments and action items and their respective dates.

   If you are hosting a meeting, you can create an agenda for it just as quickly and easily. I will often create a list of agenda items for the next meeting on each project right within my Projecteze Table, as they come up throughout my week. When the meeting time comes, it's all ready for me to print off on a separate sheet. Using a simple *copy-paste*, your agenda will include everything you need to cover, based on the key information you've been compiling in your Projecteze Table.

2) **Smart Phones, Tablets and Projecteze.** If you have a smart phone that uses Windows Mobile® 6 Professional (or later) as its operating system, you can load your Projecteze Table into your device and use the MS Word Mobile component of that operating system to take your table with you wherever you go. MS Word documents can also be opened and edited on a BlackBerry®, an iPhone®, an iPad® and many other smart phones and tablets using Documents To Go® by DataViz or Quickoffice®. These programs allow you to view, insert, and edit tables in MS Word documents. **Check the website www. OnTopOfEverything.com for the latest updates on mobile solutions for Projecteze.**

3) **References Within a Projecteze Table.** Use single handling as much as possible by filing physical documents (lists, invoices, receipts, forms, records, etc) into their own permanent location where they can and will continue to reside, *even if they require a follow-up action.* Then use a simple note in your Projecteze Table to remind you where you put those important documents when it is time to follow-up on them. This will ensure you know exactly where to look when you need to access them again. If there is no follow-up action, there will be no need for a comment in your Projecteze Table and you will have filed them once and for all into their permanent home; you may never have to source them again.

Insert references to items such as files, emails, documents, folders or forms that need to be filled out on a specific day into your Projecteze Table. Describe where you placed the associated documents and enough information that will make it easy to find them when you need them, using a brief note in the brackets at the end of your action item information packet.

As you work with this process more and more, you will become even more organized about where to place, store or archive items. These will often be project or subject files and will become your natural first place to look anyway. Arranging documents in a file chronologically makes it much easier to track down specific records. Adding notes to your Projecteze Table is especially helpful when there are items that could be filed in more than one location.

It is really rewarding to be able to read about something that requires your attention, recognizing that you made the note to yourself two months earlier very clearly describing exactly where you placed the associated documentation— all in only a few words. In a matter of seconds you know what you need to do and where the original information is located. This little technique alone has saved me countless hours of frustration and lost time.

4) **Delete a Completed Project.** When you completely finish a project, delete the entire row in your Projecteze Table. There is a wonderful feeling of accomplishment and closure that goes along with this process–similar to what you'll experience on a daily basis when you delete individual action items that have been completed.

5) **Add a New Project to a Table.** When you begin a new project, simply add a new row and start adding only the basic information–commitments and action items complete with next action dates–that is pertinent to you. Then re-sort and you're ready to stay one step ahead on your new project as well as your other ongoing projects.

6) **Clearing Cells in a Table.** If you want to clear specific information from several rows or columns in your Projecteze Table, but want to keep the rest of the information in the other rows or columns, simply highlight the information you want to clear and hit your Delete key. Presto! Those cells in your table are clear.

   If you accidentally delete some of your valuable information, use the *Edit>Undo* feature to retrace that step. If something catastrophic happens to your table, you will have the previous day's version to return to, preventing you from losing more than one day's entries.

7) **Set up Several Tables within One Projecteze Document.** This technique can be helpful when you insert additional tables at the top or bottom of your Projecteze document, that is, above or below your main Projecteze Table. If you have a large number of projects in your main Projecteze Table, you might want to place a separate stand-alone Index table *above* your main Projecteze Table. Insert Bookmarks in Your Projecteze Table (at the Project name of each row) and then insert Hyperlinks to those Bookmarks in the Index table. Clicking on the hyperlinks provides an easy way to hop around a multi-page Projecteze document.

You could also record master lists in a separate stand-alone table *below* your main Projecteze Table, for example, to capture project numbers, charge codes, contacts information or any other information that applies across all your projects. This becomes a readily available source for information that you require frequently.

8) **Projecteze as a Legal Document.** Your Projecteze Tables can be used as legal documents that will stand up as evidence in court, confirming the history concerning specific commitments that were made, by whom, when and how. Each Projecteze Table in your archive references the date within the name of the document and the electronic stamp of the MS Word document confirms the date that table was created and saved.

9) **Sort Specific Text Using the Paragraphs Sort Feature.** I have explained that for sorting your entire Projecteze Table, you must have a single flashing cursor anywhere within the table. If instead, prior to accessing the sort window, your cursor is not a single flashing cursor but covers highlighted text (even one single space or character), the sort window will give you a *Paragraphs* sort option. This indicates that MS Word thinks you want to sort just the selected text and not the entire table.

I have also described how to select each bulleted action item (three clicks of the mouse until it is all highlighted) and drag it to its proper chronological place within that cell. This is easy to do, however, you can use the *Paragraphs* sort feature in MS Word to accomplish the same thing.

The *Paragraphs* sort feature enables you to work only with the text that you specify by highlighting it. With flag dates in front of your action items in the Commitments & Action Items column, you may want to use this feature.

By having the next action date in front of the description of your action items, you can use your cursor to highlight them and then use the *Paragraphs* sort feature. It will rearrange those items in order of dates.

The following example shows the before and after of such a sort. In this example, the information packets are a list of activities that were set up for a summer vacation camping trip. They were entered into the "Camping Trip" row as they were added to the agenda for the trip so the dates are out of sequence.

| Project | Date | Prty | Commitments & Action Items |
|---------|------|------|----------------------------|
| Camping Trip | Aug 15 | 1 | • Aug 15: Pack the car<br>• Aug 16: Head to Yoho National Park<br>• Sept 5: Meet Bill & Doris at Shuswap Lake<br>• Aug 25: Meet Peg & Bill at Spirit Falls<br>• Aug 20: Call mom at home for her birthday<br>• Aug 31: Cabin booked for us at Whistler<br>• Aug 18: John to join us camping (two days) |

Highlight all of the action items with the cursor and select *Table>Sort*. It will show *Paragraphs* for your sort and will likely recognize these as being dates. If not, designate them as dates versus text or numbers in the sort window. Choose *Ascending* for the sort sequence, no header row and click *OK*.

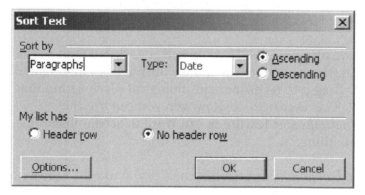

This is what you will end up with:

| Project | Date | Prty | Commitments & Action Items |
|---------|------|------|---------------------------|
| **Camping Trip** | Aug 15 | 1 | • Aug 15: Pack the car<br>• Aug 16: Head to Yoho National Park<br>• Aug 18: John to join us camping (two days)<br>• Aug 20: Call mom at home for her birthday<br>• Aug 25: Meet Peg & Bill at Spirit Falls<br>• Aug 31: Cabin booked for us at Whistler<br>• Sept 5: Meet Bill & Doris at Shuswap Lake |

As you can see, all of the individual items have been sorted according to the date at the beginning of each packet. Any packets that do not have a preceding flag date will be sorted to the top of the list.

Note: This feature does have a limitation. If you have reference dates in brackets at the end of your packets, those dates can interfere with a *Paragraphs* sort by date.

**10) Use Text Highlighting and Bold Text to Grab Attention.**
For higher priorities or more immediate action items in your Projecteze Table, consider using text highlighting and/or text bolding in the Commitments & Action Items column to make them visually stand out. I recommend that you use a bright yellow to highlight text because it is the brightest color perceived by the human eye. When printed in black and white, the yellow highlighting prints as a light grey, doesn't use a lot of ink, and doesn't interfere with reading the text it surrounds.

For special cases, you can use either highlighting or bolding to make specific text stand out. Obviously, a bold, highlighted text *really* jumps out.

Alternate highlight colors could be used to indicate different priorities or types of action items (such as business or personal), but it's a good idea to use text highlighting sparingly. If you get carried away with it, you'll lose the impact and will simply end up with an overwhelming multi-colored page with lots of bolded text. It will look confusing and will not be easy to read.

Alternatively, you could use highlighting for one type of priority (e.g. urgent items) and bold text for another (e.g. time sensitivity). Again, this is where the flexibility of the Projecteze system allows you to be creative and customize your table. Just be sure to keep simplicity in the forefront of your mind.

11) **Embedding Links to Other Documents.** You can embed links to documents that you need to access frequently. Opening them is only one click away at any time. The caveat here is that links will lose their connection and stop working if the name or location of the document they are linked to changes. If the name and location of the linked document is likely to remain the same, this can be a very powerful solution that does not increase the size of your Projecteze Table.

To insert a link, use the menu *Insert>Hyperlink*. Once the link is inserted into your Projecteze Table, hold your mouse over the link, hold down the *Ctrl* key if you're using a PC (not required on a Mac®), and click on the link. Instantly you will be connected to the document.
Now, that's efficient!

12) **Embedding Portions of Other Documents.** You can embed a portion of a spreadsheet right into your Projecteze Table if you need to work with a larger group of numbers and to have the full functionality of a spreadsheet readily available.

For example, with a link you can embed an MS Excel graph from another file, into your Projecteze Table. If the data and graph in the source MS Excel file are changed, you can easily update the graph in your Projecteze Table with a quick right-mouse click and selecting *Update Link*. To do this:

a. Open an existing or blank MS Excel spreadsheet

b. Highlight the range of the spreadsheet you want to insert into your Projecteze Table. *Copy* this area.

c. Go to your Projecteze Table and place your cursor where you want to place that portion of the spreadsheet.

d. Use the MS Word menus *Edit>Paste Special*

e. In the MS Word *Paste Special* pop-up window, select *Paste link*, and *Microsoft Office Excel Worksheet Object* from the list of options. This will embed the range you have copied from your MS Excel document into your Projecteze document while maintaining a link to the original MS Excel document. [Selecting *Paste* versus *Paste link* will place that portion of the spreadsheet where you want it but you will not be able to update it with changes made to the source file.]

f. Option: If you don't want the numbers in this spreadsheet to be readily visible within your Projecteze document, additionally select the *Display as icon* box. This will create the spreadsheet in your table but it will only be shown as an icon, which might be necessary for confidentiality on a printed version of your table.

g. Click *OK*

Once embedded, you can double click on the spreadsheet or the icon in your Projecteze Table to open MS Excel and manipulate the data with full MS Excel functionality. I have embedded an MS Excel spreadsheet here to show you what it can look like:

| Division | 1st Qtr | 2nd Qtr | 3rd Qtr | 4th Qtr | Total |
|----------|---------|---------|---------|---------|---------|
| East | 15,000 | 18,000 | 22,000 | 10,000 | 65,000 |
| West | 18,000 | 21,000 | 15,000 | 16,000 | 70,000 |
| North | 29,000 | 24,000 | 25,000 | 18,000 | 96,000 |
| South | 12,000 | 15,000 | 18,000 | 15,000 | 60,000 |
| Total: | 74,000 | 78,000 | 80,000 | 59,000 | 291,000 |

The MS Excel spreadsheet in your Projecteze Table can be updated whenever the original source document is modified.

13) **Embedding Complete Documents.** Perhaps an even more powerful solution is to embed complete files right into your Projecteze Table for quick access to frequently used reference materials.

This will cause your Projecteze document to increase in size by the size of the embedded (second) file. If you plan to embed several or large secondary files, you will probably be better off inserting links to them instead.

During the embedding process, you can choose whether or not to have an umbilical cord in the way of a link to the source of each embedded secondary file. Instead of having just an embedded link, you will have an embedded file with a link back to the source document.

Embedding a linked secondary document into your Projecteze Table enables both the source document and the secondary file in your table to always be the same. You can edit either one and the changes will be reflected in the other, as long as they are on the same network and can access each other. Now, that's even *more* efficient!

As you change the name of your Projecteze document each day (adjusting the date, as recommended in Chapter Two), your embedded file will still retain its link with the source secondary file. It will not retain the link if the name of the source secondary file is changed.

Embedding secondary files into your Projecteze Table can be very beneficial if you need access to documents whose file names don't change very often and for which you need to maintain a link for editing right from your Projecteze Table. Alternatively, embedding a secondary file without a link can be a great way to make reference materials, such as a pdf document, easily accessible.

If the source secondary file is updated and saved as a newly named document, perhaps with the more current date for it, your embedded file will not be linked to the newer version but will still be linked to the previously dated source secondary file. You will need to re-embed this file to have a link to the newer version.

I want to emphasize that each embedded file increases the size of your Projecteze Table by the size of the embedded file. You will need to manage this closely to ensure your Projecteze Table does not become so large that it is unwieldy and takes a long time just to open. MS Word documents tend to be small in size and this is one of the benefits of working with them.

To embed secondary files into your Projecteze Table:

a. Open your Projecteze document and click into your table where you want to place the embedded file.

b. Click *Insert>Object>*tab *Create from File.*

c. Use *Browse* to locate the secondary file you want to embed (word processing document, spreadsheet, image, graph, media clip) and click *Insert.*

Linking. By selecting *Link to file,* any changes made to the source document of a secondary file will automatically be made to the file embedded in your Table, and visa versa. By not selecting *Link to file,* changes made to the source of a secondary file will not be made in your Projecteze Table.

d. Selecting *Display as icon* will insert an icon into your Projecteze Table that represents the contents of the embedded file.

e. By not selecting *Display as icon,* the contents of the secondary file will be embedded right into your Projecteze Table.

f. Click *OK.* Double clicking on the icon or file will open it from inside your Projecteze Table.

## 14) Embedding a Smaller Table within Your Projecteze Table.

Let's say you have a group of telephone numbers or budget code numbers you need to access regularly and easily— sufficiently few that you don't need to create a separate list or a stand-alone table. You can actually insert those numbers right inside your Projecteze Table for easy reference by using a separate smaller table that is embedded within it.

This can be a very powerful way to group information. You could insert a table under the project title in the first column of each project (row) in which to record numbers such as the project number, contract number or purchase order number.

Not only can you insert a table within your Projecteze Table but you can sort just this smaller embedded table on its own as well, just the way you've been sorting your overall Projecteze Table, as long as your cursor is somewhere inside the smaller table. And when you sort your entire Projecteze Table, the embedded table gets properly sorted along with the row it is in.

When your cursor is inside any cell within your main Projecteze Table, you can insert another table into that spot and specify the number of columns and rows it requires. Use the menus *Table>Insert>Table*.

Working with our camping trip example, I needed easy access to the telephone numbers of the people we were going to meet during the trip. I entered them into an embedded table that I could sort by Contact. For the trip, I could print just this row and take it along for the itinerary and contact telephone numbers. A *copy-paste* of just this row onto a blank page worked very well. Get in the car, kids!

| Project | Date | Prty | Commitments & Action Items |
|---------|------|------|----------------------------|
| **Camping Trip** | Aug 15 | 1 | • Aug 15: Pack the car<br>• Aug 16: Head to Yoho National Park<br>• Aug 18: John to join us camping (two days)<br>• Aug 20: Call mom at home for her birthday<br>• Aug 25: Meet Peg & Bill at Spirit Falls<br>• Aug 31: Cabin booked for us at Whistler<br>• Sept 5: Meet Bill & Doris at Shuswap Lake |

| Contact | Cell Phone |
|---------|-----------|
| Bill & Doris, Shuswap Lake | (403) 537-8965 |
| John | (403) 765-8974 |
| Mom | (403) 278-5461 |
| Peg & Bill | (250) 768-5998 |
| Whistler Cabin | (250) 316-6486 |
| Yoho Campsite | (250) 341-1517 |

Using these 14 additional tips and practical techniques will enhance your use of the Projecteze system.

Here's a final tip that I highly recommend: after a month of using the Projecteze system, re-read this book. This will help you fully integrate all the information into your Projecteze Table, and it will serve as a refresher on all the great ideas we've talked about. It will really bring home how you can fully apply this system and help to make sure you are getting everything you can out of it.

# VIII

## Projecteze For Home

*Home is a place you grow up wanting to leave,*
*and grow old wanting to get back to.*
—John Ed Pearce

Staying on top of everything means staying on top of your home life as well. I find nothing more satisfying than to be able to walk into my house and know exactly where everything is and what needs to be done in order to stay on top of ongoing family activities and household maintenance requirements. By applying the Projecteze method to my personal life, this is easy to accomplish.

I'm sure that if you're like most people, the minute you come in the door after a long day at work you're used to having something new come at you from a child or a spouse. "The car is making funny noises." "I need help with my school project." "The roof is leaking." Many of these commitments need to be and can be dealt with immediately, but others will need to be scheduled in with your other ongoing commitments that require your attention. From scheduling and tracking home maintenance items to highlighting personal interests and hobbies, all of your action items, urgent or not, can be captured and managed in one personal or home Projecteze Table.

Once you set up and begin to use a home Projecteze Table, you'll discover that it becomes not only a handy reminder of routine chores and recurring events, but you can also use it to keep track of your personal interests and goals. The real bonus from feeling on top of all your home-related projects is that you can start taking time for those things that bring peace and enjoyment to your life.

I find that I usually only need to refer to my personal Projecteze Table once or twice a week. I'll often transfer only the items coming up for that week onto a separate (perhaps handwritten) list for reference throughout the week. At the end of the week, I'll update my table and get ready for the following week. Projecteze for home lets me capture everything critical or of personal interest for reference when the time is right for me.

 Laurence Seton © | Projecteze Inc.

My own personal Projecteze Table includes the following rows:

## Spring Household Maintenance

Using conventional paper systems for many years, I found I would have to rewrite the same list of things to do each spring to prepare the house and yard for the summer. Now, I just list them all in this row of my Projecteze Table with the Date column set for sometime in the spring. When this row bubbles up to the top of my table, I'm reminded about exactly what I need to do.

As I complete these tasks, I do not delete them but shade (grey) them over. Once I've completed them all, I'll remove all of the shading and change the date to springtime of the following year. That will take the row back to the bottom of my table and out of my way until I need to see it again. I no longer have to keep re-writing the same list of things to do into my personal calendar every year.

## Fall Household Maintenance

I apply the same method in the fall as I did for the Spring Household Maintenance. The reason I have a separate row for the fall is because the tasks are different from those I do in the spring.

## Household—General

Here I list all the changes we want to make to our home or things we want to buy for it such as: specific furniture we want, flooring to be replaced, landscaping to do, or painting to be done. I list anything and everything that pertains to the house— excluding the repeated Spring and Fall maintenance items. For each item listed here, I'll record an approximate single budget figure for future reference because I usually price it out when I add it to my table. This helps me remember what that approximate cost will be by the time I actually get around to doing the task or making a purchase.

Family

In this row, I list specific commitments that anyone in the family has. This doesn't replace the monthly calendar on the kitchen wall—that still works very well for recording and staying on top of everyone's regular appointments such as swimming lessons, karate, hockey, football, or baseball as well as any medical or dental appointments.

What the Projecteze Table is especially good for is listing special family items such as helping a son or daughter schedule the components of a larger school project, or listing all the details you have to tend to in order to get your son or daughter ready for that school band trip to Europe. This could present the perfect opportunity for teaching your children the Projecteze system.

Automobiles

Next to our homes, our biggest investments are usually vehicles. There are many issues associated with purchasing and servicing vehicles.

Questions that guide what I place in this row are: What will the odometer reading be for each of my vehicles when they have to go in for their next servicing? What is the expected cost? What additional major automobile maintenance items are coming up? (tires, alignment, etc.) When is the insurance due on my vehicles, what am I paying, and where is the policy located? What other vehicles do I want to take out for a test drive, or buy? I'll also record my license plate numbers (and in some cases the VIN numbers) in case I require them for reference or for booking service appointments.

Laurence Seton © | Projecteze Inc.

## Financial

Because I manage my detailed personal budget in a spreadsheet, this is the row for reminding me about special or annual tasks related to my financial matters such as critical dates for reviewing investments, re-financing loans that are coming due, paying property taxes, or contacting my accountant about doing my corporate and personal income tax returns which happen at different times of the year.

## Internet

Here I record website addresses or online articles I want to check out, but due to time constraints, I will have to return to at a later time. Often I will bookmark website addresses right in my browser, along with the thousands of other addresses I have in there, but for those very special sites that I know I want to come back to, I'll paste the addresses into this row of my Projecteze Table. That way I know they won't get lost and they're easy to access with a simple *Ctrl + click* on the link.

## Home Computer

In this row I keep notes about new computer programs I want to purchase and learn, or special computer-related projects such as organizing my digital photos. I make notes to myself about regular computer maintenance, software upgrades, and data back-up tasks that I don't want to forget about. I'll also list computer books I want to read here. Because this is a large topic on its own, I'll include computer-related books here rather than in my "Reading" row.

## Hobbies

From describing items I want to pursue for my existing hobbies to listing completely new hobbies I want to explore, this becomes a wonderful place to capture fun stuff that I want to spend my free time on such as shops I may have seen on my travels that I want to return to someday. These items are included here.

## Guitar

One of my personal goals is to learn how to play the guitar well; therefore, it gets its own row. I include steps I plan to take, instruction books to acquire, names and contact numbers of local guitar instructors, and best of all, a list of the guitars I've been eyeing.

## Shopping

This is my wish list—in order of priority or desire—containing all the items I want to purchase but which I can't justify buying just yet. When someone asks me what I want for my birthday, I've got a list all ready. Once I decide on the guitar I want to get, I can add it into my Shopping row as a future purchase or, finances permitting, drop it right into my detailed budget as a formally planned expenditure.

## Miscellaneous

This row is a catch-all for other items such as preparing our annual family Christmas card (in November) so it's ready to send out in December.

## Reading

As a writer and an avid reader, this row contains a list of books I have on my horizon—books that have been recommended to me by friends or that I've heard are worthwhile.

## Travel

As a family, we enjoy travel. In this row I record ideas about where we might travel to next, perhaps with a brief description of locations to include on each trip. This is a row that receives regular attention as I read various articles about those far-off destinations. I'll also include a ballpark budget figure for each trip.

*This is my own personal Projecteze Table for Dec 17, 2008:*

| Area | Date | Issues & Actions |
|---|---|---|
| **Internet** | Dec 17 | • Jan 10: Check out next edition of Consumer Reports<br>• Jim's Vintage Guitars: www.jimsguitars.com<br>• Rarities of the World: www.stacks.com<br>• Mt Kobau Star Party: www.mksp.ca |
| **Shopping** | Dec 19 | • Get new soles put onto black boots<br>• Buy scarf to go with my new overcoat<br>• "Planet Earth" in Blu-ray<br>• Air chair for Shuswap cabin ($1,500)<br>• Two new bicycles ($2,000) |
| **Reading** | Dec 19 | Books to buy:<br>• *P-47 Pilots: The Fighter-Bomber Boys* (by Tom Glenn)<br>• *Thunderbolt: Memoirs of a World War II Fighter Pilot* (by Marvin Bledsoe)<br>• *Slide:ology: The Art and Science of Creating Great Presentations* (by Nancy Duarte)<br>• *Reality Check* (by Guy Kawasaki)<br>• *Made to Stick: Why Some Ideas Survive and Others Die* (by Chip & Dan Heath)<br>• *The Tao of Now: Daily Wisdom from Mystics, Sages, Poets, and Saints* (by Josh Baran)<br>• *Radiant Mind: Awakening Unconditioned Awareness* (by Peter Fenner) |
| **Financial** | Dec 20 | • Dec 20: Prepare budget template for next year<br>• Feb 5: Buy RRSPs<br>• March 10: Call Brock to set up our personal Income Tax Returns |
| **Home Computer** | Dec 21 | • Dec 21: Learn the camcorder and new mic<br>• Dec 21: Learn how to use Apple Remote on my iPhone™<br>• Keep an eye out for Documents To Go® for the iPhone™; possibly coming out soon. I'm set up to receive an email when it's ready (Sept/08) I completed their survey (Nov 13)<br>• Read: *Mac OS X*® - *The Missing Manual*<br>• Read: *OS X Leopard*® - *Killer Apps*<br>• Digitize all of our slides; need special slide scanner ($800) |
| **Travel** | Feb 1/09 | • Dominican Republic (1 week; $5,000)<br>• Greece (6 wks; $25,000)<br>• Thailand (6 wks; $20,000)<br>• Berlin & Germany (3 wks; $15,000)<br>• Train trip in Canada (1 wk; $5,000) |
| **Automobiles & Motorcycles**<br><br>TXR 780:<br>Next oil chg: 22,000<br>PZE 009:<br>Next oil chg: 45,000 | Feb 10/09 | • Check out the new Ford Mustang<br>• Check out the Nissan GT-R<br>• Test ride a Star Raider S<br>• Test ride a Kawasaki Vulcan |

| Area | Date | Issues & Actions |
|------|------|------------------|
| **Guitar** | Feb 25/09 | • Start playing again<br>• Finish learning the amp<br>• Find a good teacher; UofC student?<br>• Buy a Variax 700; & get Miles to set it up<br>• Martin HD-28V acoustical guitar + electronics ($4,000) |
| **Miscellaneous** | March 15/09 | • March 15/09: Register 40 PDUs with PMI; category 2F<br>• Nov/2009: Prepare Christmas card |
| **Spring House Mtce** | Apr 01/09 | • Clean the barbecue<br>• Turn off outside taps, turn taps in basement on and put hoses out<br>• Clean out the garage<br>• Defrost the garage fridge & freezer<br>• Wash the front deck<br>• Wash house windows<br>• Turn on outside lights timer<br>• Put deck chairs out<br>• May: Wash & wax (detail) both cars |
| **Household** | Apr 10/09 | • Spring/09: New (natural gas) barbecue ($990)<br>• May 30/09: Get carpets cleaned<br>• New master bedroom furniture ($7,000)<br>• Get weekly yard mtce set up ($1,000/yr)<br>• Water softener system ($4,000)<br>• Two new office chairs for home ($2,500)<br>• Get the house interior painted ($10,000)<br>• Replace flooring throughout the house ($20,000)<br>• New kitchen knives ($1,000)<br>• Frame picture from Thailand ($200)<br>• Digital satellite service? ($200)<br>• Create library in main floor room ($300)<br>• Zero gravity chairs (2) for the basement ($3,500)<br>• Bankboard shuffleboard table ($2,000)<br>• Lonechild print framed ($200)<br>• Sheepskin mattress cover ($1,000)<br>• New front door foyer carpet ($2,000)<br>• Get an irrigation system put in ($4,000) |
| **Fall House Mtce** | Oct 13/09 | • Put deck chairs away<br>• Fireplace cleaned<br>• Lubricate garage door<br>• Rake & clean up the yard<br>• Put hoses away, turn off two blue taps in basement ceiling & open outside taps for the winter<br>• Get furnace & humidifier serviced |

Laurence Seton © | Projecteze Inc.

As you read the descriptions in the rows I have in my home Projecteze Table, you probably imagined how you could add other rows to reflect aspects of your own home life. These could be rows for personal goals; entertainment; birthday and anniversary lists; electronic clipping files for a specific topic; summer cabin and boat maintenance—or anything else you want to track in your Personal Projecteze Table.

You may also want to create a specific Projecteze Table to help you manage larger personal projects such as a home renovation, a large family reunion, or a complicated medical treatment plan. My method is flexible enough and simple enough that if you use it once for these special personal projects, you'll likely return to Projecteze to manage other multi-faceted family issues or events.

For example, Projecteze proved invaluable when our family moved from one city to another. Over a fifteen-year period, we moved three times, each time to another city. For every move, there was a tremendous number of details that had to be tracked and completed.

For the third move, I used the Projecteze system to compile all the lists I had on how to prepare for a move provided by various moving companies and lawyers. This time, I managed the whole process electronically with all the pertinent details at my fingertips.

There were multiple recurring legal, financial, logistical and overall coordination aspects for each move. Each one of these topic areas was assigned a separate row in my personal Projecteze Table. Eventually and toward the end of a move, as the number of remaining tasks dropped off, all of those rows were compiled into one remaining row. The next step was to create new rows to capture all of the tasks for setting up the new residence (e.g. get all the locks re-keyed, set up accounts with the utility companies, send out personal change of address notifications, etc.)

The Projecteze system let me flow seamlessly from one stage of my life to the next without missing a beat. You have to realize that I didn't have to create multiple Projecteze Tables, one for each stage of the move. Instead, it was all done with just one Projecteze Table that continued to evolve through the entire process.

This final move progressed at a more comfortable and orderly pace than the others, and nothing was missed, going from a well-established home life with a consistent daily pattern to the upheaval of moving to a new job and new residence in another city and back to an orderly home life with a consistent daily pattern.

You will also be able to respond with the utmost efficiency no matter what life throws at you when you use Projecteze to help manage the daily routines and challenges in your personal life.

# IX

## Projecteze For School

*The whole purpose of education
is to turn mirrors into windows.*
    −Sydney J. Harris

Each year September brings change and new experiences for students and teachers. For younger students, summer is over and the two months off has come to an end; for older students, it's nice to let go of four months of working and return to campus. The start of a new school year means meeting new friends, taking on new challenges and, eventually, facing the less appealing prospect of having to hand in assignments, submit papers and write exams. For teachers, the beginning of the academic year means scheduling units and testing, coordinating curriculum, designing assignments, and juggling teaching with administrative duties.

Right from the beginning, the success of any project is closely correlated to how well the project is set up and managed. Every new school year, students and teachers need to manage several projects simultaneously as they strive for success. Whatever the learning task, Projecteze can be a tremendously helpful tool for both students and teachers.

In this chapter, I'll concentrate on using Projecteze at school from a student perspective, though teachers will also be able to benefit substantially from the Projecteze method.

My memories of school are, for the most, very good. I recall easing back into high school after summer. The pace was very manageable, though it required some sense of self-discipline to be able to complete assignments and prepare for exams for five courses. Each year, the pressure continued to build as the semester unfolded, culminating at the end of my senior year with an exam for each course that was worth 60% of the final mark.

Post-secondary education was enjoyable too. It brought with it more responsibilities, coupled with a tremendously liberating sense of freedom to be able to do what I wanted to do, whenever I wanted to do it (within reason). That sense of liberation, however, was short-lived as I found out the first day when I received, for each course, an outline, a list of books to buy and read that semester, dates for mid-term exams and, often, the first assignment. With a fuse that was lit the first day back, it was very easy to fall behind as I chased an ever-increasing wave of homework and studying. Oh, how I wish I had Projecteze during those days.

Having developed the Projecteze system, I've discovered its flexibility is perfect for students.

**High School and Beyond**

*I have never let my schooling interfere with my education.*
—Mark Twain

James is an average Grade 10 student who is getting used to the heavier workload associated with high school. He has done relatively well in school in the past but finds school is starting to become a bit more challenging because he has to be more responsible about completing his assignments. He finds he has more homework, and the effort he has to put into his assignments is greater than what he was used to. And from what he's heard, it doesn't get any easier.

James' father learned about the Projecteze system and thought James might benefit from it; so he introduced him to the system. After reading the book and setting up his table, James referred to it daily as he entered new assignments, chapters he had to read, reports to write, and dates for his exams. Within one week, James had set up his Projecteze Table for school. It looked like this:

| Subject | Date | Prty | Homework |
|---------|------|------|----------|
| **Biology 10** | Oct 16 | 1 | • Oct 16: Read chapter 6 & assignment #1; due Oct 18<br>• Read pamphlet from fish hatchery<br>• Oct 20: Study for exam<br>• Oct 21: Field trip to fish hatchery<br>• Oct 23: Exam |
| **Math 10** | Oct 17 | 1 | • Read chapter 5 & do quiz at end of chapter<br>• Oct 19 & 20: Study for exam on chapters 3 & 4<br>• Oct 21: Exam —chapters 3 & 4 |
| **Recreation** | Oct 17 | 3 | • Get waiver signed by Mom for basketball team trips; due Oct 22<br>• Nov 15: Sign up to take life saving course |

| Subject | Date | Prty | Homework |
|---|---|---|---|
| **Shop Class** | Oct 18 | 2 | • Go in after classes to work on woodworking project<br>• Oct 20: Check with Mom about doing the kayaks ($150.00 per student)<br>• Oct 23: Mr. Blayney is having a meeting (4:30 pm) for anyone interested in building fiberglass kayaks —an after school project |
| **Physics 10** | Oct 19 | 2 | • Oct 19: Read chapter 12<br>• Oct 19: Group assignment —meet at Jim⊡s at 7:00 pm<br>• Nov 1: Group assignment due to be handed in for marking<br>• Nov 5: Science Fair —Bill & I to host booth<br>• Nov 10: Exam |
| **Chemistry 10** | Oct 21 | 1 | • Start researching info on exothermic reactions<br>• Do assignment 5<br>• Oct 24: Assignment #5 due<br>• Oct 27: Lab 3 report due<br>• Nov 13: Exam —chapters 5 to 8<br>• Nov 22: Report on Exothermic Reactions is due (2,000 words)<br>• Course reading, for the week of:<br>  Oct 25: Chapter 7<br>  Nov 1: Chapter 8<br>  Nov 8: Chapters 11 & 12<br>  Nov 15: Chapters 13 & 14<br>  Nov 30: Chapter 16 |

Throughout the school year, James stuck with his Projecteze Table and it served him very well. James completed the year with excellent marks, though he couldn't quite figure out why his mom and dad thought it was such a big deal. It seemed easy to him because he was always on top of his school work, he could see exactly what was coming at him every week, and for several weeks, and every step of the way, he knew what he needed to be working on next. Everything just seemed to fall into place.

James continued to use the Projecteze system throughout the rest of high school, achieving high grades every year. This set him up for post-secondary education and beyond. In fact, being on top of everything set him up for life.

## Off To Post-Secondary School

Helping my own daughter reach her goal of being admitted to a university provided a perfect opportunity to use Projecteze as we worked together toward that goal. We knew that reaching it would be a long process. Viewing it as a project, we began managing the components to ensure her successful application and admission to the school of her choice.

My daughter, Christy, was a very determined student during high school. When she brought her report cards home in Grade 10, her mom and I could see she was getting some very good marks. Watching her at home, I knew how hard she worked on her homework and studying. Of course, I was very proud of her, but it also motivated me to help her as much as I could.

Early in her Grade 11 year, I sat down with Christy and together we made a deal: I would work with her and help her submit applications for a post-secondary education if she would continue to work really hard at high school and get the best marks she could. For the next two years, she continued to work diligently and I dove right into helping coordinate the process of selecting a school and helping her submit the best applications possible.

Christy certainly kept her part of the bargain in high school. She was one of only five students out of a class of 250 who received a prestigious award for maintaining a 3.75 grade point average throughout her high school years. A wonderful achievement.

The following series of Projecteze Tables shows how I was able to keep both of us well organized during the process of applying for her admission to university. The project evolved in three stages that are described in the following three tables:

1. Prepare to apply to post-secondary schools during the first half of Grade 11.

2. Apply to specific post-secondary schools early in Grade 12.

3. Choose one school and prepare to attend (late in Grade 12).

In the following illustrations, you can appreciate the complexity of the process and how Christy and I were able to collaborate as we moved toward her goal.

*Prepare to apply to post-secondary schools*
*during the first half of Grade 11:*

After making our pact, our first objective was to set up the parameters for this two-year project. This was the time when we worked together to:

a. Prepare a summary of her academic records.

b. Confirm what courses she needed to take each year while still in high school and the grades she should be striving for.

c. Learn about what scholarships might be available for her and how to apply for them.

d. Start to learn about and understand the options available for financing her education.

The first table below pertained to simply preparing to apply for post-secondary education. It shows what we were doing and tracking during the first half of her Grade 11 year. In many of the rows you will see that the Projecteze Table also started to pull in important dates for the following year. It was never too early to start capturing all of the key dates we needed to be aware of in these early days. The dates are all listed chronologically within each row. If a date seems out of sequence within a row, it's because it applied to the following year.

| Component | Date | Prty | Actions & Deadlines |
|---|---|---|---|
| **General** | Oct 1/97 | 3 | • Oct 1: Read the *Guidebook for High School Graduates*<br>• Dec 1: Christy to apply for an employment number |
| **Academic Records** | Oct 15/97 | 2 | • Oct 15: Prepare summary of high school marks<br>• Jan 1: Work with Christy to prepare her resume, capturing all of her accomplishments to date<br>• Mar 1: Tabulate a summary of all high school credits earned thus far plus those projected; including work experience requirements vs. work experience completed<br>• Nov 3: Christy to update her resume to include: Leadership Forum, instructing synchronized swimming & anything else that will help to present her capabilities |

| Component | Date | Prty | Actions & Deadlines |
|---|---|---|---|
| **University Applications** | Nov 1/97 | 2 | • Nov 1: Read & summarize write-ups on each school from:<br>  A) *Maclean's Guide To Universities*, and<br>  B) *Real Guide to Canadian Universities*<br>• Jan 1: Discuss Christy's preferred schools with her<br>• Feb 1: Write to the selected universities for general admission information.<br>• March 1: Receive responses from selected universities; with confirmation of admission requirements for each school<br>• Christy & I to read through information received from each school<br>• Sept 1: Confirm the list of schools Christy is most interested in attending<br>• Sept 1: Order Calendars from the selected schools; especially McGill, UBC, U of Alberta; (already have U of Calgary)<br>• Oct 1: Begin collecting application forms required for scholarships & admission from each of the selected schools |
| **Financing** | Nov 1/97 | 2 | • Nov 1: Contact Crown Publications to get a copy of *Financial Opportunities For Students Resource Book* & any other information on financial assistance for students<br>• Nov 10: Download and review standard student loan application forms |
| **Scholarships** | Nov 1/97 | 2 | • Nov 1: Set up a Projecteze table for tracking all scholarships applied for and awarded (beginning with the Passport to Education)<br>• Jan 1: Buy latest edition of book *Winning Scholarships* by Michael J Howell<br>• Feb 1: Update scholarship dates in Projecteze table with appropriate targets described in the Howell book<br>• Mar 1: Update Projecteze table to include detailed specifics from each school based on the information we receive<br>• July 1: Christy to arrange to get transcripts from MBSS forwarded to U of Calgary & U of Alberta for the *Excellence Scholarships Program*<br>• Oct 1: Investigate any and all local community, service clubs (Rotary, etc) & business bursaries or scholarships that may be available; discuss with school counselor<br>• Nov 8: Make a list of people to approach for letters of reference. [Teachers—especially if known 2 to 3 yrs & who teach in Christy's areas of interest]<br>• Nov 8: Compile & update background information to be used for all scholarship applications; resume, transcripts, etc<br>• Nov 8: Send out letters asking for references; letter with a copy of Christy's resume. |
| **High School Courses**<br><br>**(MBSS)** | Dec 15/97 | 1 | • Dec 15: Review Grade 12 courses with Christy and confirm what she will be registering in<br>Next year:<br>• Nov 2: Christy to ensure she is registered for all Provincial Exams she plans to write in Nov, Jan, April & June.<br>• Nov 2: Christy to confirm the following two items at school:<br>  1) Credits for her Grade 11 Athletics Council work?<br>  2) Credits for a) additional work experience, b) job shadowing and c) Medical Leadership Forum<br>• Nov 13: Transcript Verification Report (TVR) is issued by the government to schools in late November, confirming graduation requirements; review to confirm it is accurate. |

Christy and I did some general research on post-secondary schools over those first few months in her Grade 11 year by reading periodicals and reports such as *Maclean's Guide To Universities*. As described in the "University Applications" row above, in January of her Grade 11 year, Christy and I sat down together to narrow down the list of schools she was most interested in. She selected the following six schools from across Canada:

1) McGill University (Montréal, Québec)

2) McMaster University (Hamilton, Ontario)

3) Queens University (Kingston, Ontario)

4) University of Alberta (Edmonton, Alberta)

5) University of British Columbia (Vancouver, British Columbia)

6) University of Calgary (Calgary, Alberta)

Then we wrote to these six schools, asking for general information about the school and admission requirements. Christy and I went through this information between March and July of that year. In the following September, at the beginning of her Grade 12 year and as described in the "University Applications" row above, we sat down together again to get her to narrow down the list to only the schools she was really interested in. The list didn't get much shorter though—we were still looking at five schools. This did take us into the next stage of getting more detailed information about each of these schools, the programs and courses they offered, and specific admission requirements for each program.

*Apply to specific post-secondary schools early in Grade 12:*

Even though this example is set up in stages, and I'm showing you the stages in three separate Projecteze Tables, I want you to understand that the entire time I was really working with one–*and only one*–Projecteze Table. It simply evolved as we progressed through these stages. Items and rows were deleted while new items and rows were added. Just like the example I describe in Chapter Eight to illustrate how I applied Projecteze for our moves from one city to another, this was a single living table that carried us through the entire process.

Early in Christy's Grade 12 year and immediately after narrowing her choice down to five schools, we wrote to those schools to request admissions application forms, information on scholarship requirements and course calendars. As the responses came in, I would simply create a new row for each school and transfer key annual dates into our Projecteze Table. Instead of having to continually rummage through the individual calendars, we had all of the critical dates and information right at our fingertips.

Christy and I read through all the calendars. Wanting to enhance her chances of being accepted, we prepared and mailed applications to each of the five schools for early admission that would be granted before she had actually finished high school.

The table below shows the dates when early admission applications were due. We knew that we should hear back from each school approximately one month after the deadline. Concurrently we also had to submit housing applications for some of the schools because they were due before we would hear back as to whether or not she had been accepted into the school.

Notice that I chose to drop the Priority column because the tasks were more spread out across weeks and months so it wasn't as critical a parameter for us.

| Component | Date | Actions & Deadlines |
|---|---|---|
| **University of British Columbia** (Vancouver, British Columbia) | Nov 23/98 | • Nov 23: Request & submit housing application for UBC<br>• Jan 5: Return application for housing at UBC (They will send a letter confirming date of receipt and rates); due Feb 2 (first come, first served)<br>• Jan 10: Tell MBSS Counselors you would like to be considered for the UBC USP awards; so they will send your name & grades to UBC [must have applied for Early Admission to UBC to be eligible for a USP award]; c/w resume for consideration on others as well.<br>• Jan 13: Submit entrance application (via the internet); ask high school to send statements of interim & final grades.<br>• Feb 1: Housing application deadline (first come, first served)<br>• Feb 10: *Major Entrance Scholarship* application forms become available (due April 15); must be nominated by the high school<br>• Feb 10: Confirm that MBSS Counselor has sent latest transcript to UBC<br>• Feb 28: Deadline for early applications (can apply via the internet)<br>• Mar 2: Housing spots are assigned (higher priority if outside the lower mainland)<br>• Mar 25: *Affiliation Scholarship & Bursary* application forms are available (due May 15 & June 30)<br>• Apr 15: *Major Entrance Scholarship* applications due; for both renewable and non-renewable scholarships (must be nominated by high school)<br>• Apr 30: Normal applications deadline<br>• May 15: *Affiliation Scholarship & Bursary* applications are due<br>• May 15: Early admission confirmations are sent out<br>• May 26: Send $100 fee before May 30, in order to have access to telephone registration capabilities on June 1.<br>• Jun 1: June 1 - July 15: Registration for courses by telephone or internet<br>• Jun 15: *Major Entrance Scholarship* decisions mailed are out<br>• Jun 15: Residence room assignments are mailed out<br>• Jun 30: *Affiliation Scholarship & Bursary* applications are due<br>• Jul 15: Last day for completing course registrations.<br>• Jul 15: Deadline for receipt of transcripts<br>• Sep 1: *General Bursary* application forms are available<br>• Oct 1 *General Bursary* applications are due |
| **University Applications** | Nov 27/98 | • Nov 27: Visit the web sites of the schools Christy is most interested in for preview of deadlines, etc.<br>• Jan 14: Apply to write the *Language Proficiency Index Test* (LPI); not req'd if English mark is >85%? (the test is written in March); $39.00<br>• Feb 10: Send new copy of transcript w/letter to all universities.<br>• May 1: Fill out *Post-Secondary Institution Choices Form* at school to state where you want to have final transcripts sent in early August. (plus to send interim grades to BC universities in May if you're on Early Admissions Program)<br>• May 5: The government again issues Transcript Verification Report (TVR) to schools in early May confirming graduation requirements; review to confirm it is accurate.<br>• Jul 6: Write to all references to tell them how you are making out (school chosen, etc.)<br>• Aug 1: Early August: Transcripts for Grades 11 & 12 are sent out to student plus universities selected in March (For Provincials, they list: school%, prov exam%, final%, & final letter grade per course; 3.0 gr pt avg = Honours Standing indicated on transcript) |

Laurence Seton © | Projecteze Inc.

| Component | Date | Actions & Deadlines |
|---|---|---|
| **University of Calgary** (Calgary, Alberta) | Nov 28/98 | • Nov 28: Submit application to U of C for: 1) Outstanding Achievement Awards, and 2) Matriculation Awards (both are due Dec 1)<br>• Nov 28: Submit entrance application (required by Dec 1 to maintain Scholars Advantage benefits)<br>• Apr 10: "Outstanding Achievement Scholarships" awarded<br>• Apr 20: Mail in Residence registration (deadline for guaranteed room registration = May 3; cost = $25.00).<br>• Apr 20: Send $100 fee before April 30, in order to have access to May 3 - 17 telephone registration capabilities.<br>• May 1: Normal applications deadline<br>• May 3 - 17: Advanced course registration by telephone.<br>• May 25: *Matriculation Awards* issued<br>• May 30: Housing application deadline<br>• Jun 30: Deadline for receipt of transcripts<br>• Jul 1: Deadline for advanced parking applications. |
| **Scholarships** | Dec 2/98 | • Dec 3: Review and summarize general information on scholarships<br>• Dec 3, 7:00 pm, Dec 3: Scholarship Info & Support Meeting, MBSS<br>• Dec 11: Do search on net for other scholarships<br>• Dec 15: Contact the Financial Aid Offices at the selected universities for info about scholarships & awards, as well as application deadlines. (request application forms)<br>• Dec 16: Gather letters of reference<br>• Jan 7: Contact private scholarship funds targeted to request guidelines, deadlines & application forms.<br>• Jan 15: Ask for the Principals Scholarship application form from the MBSS office<br>• Jan 21: Look for COBSS Bursaries application forms<br>• Feb 5: Draft introduction letter (for COBSS, & other?)<br>• Apr 30: Dr. David Clarke Bursary application deadline<br>• May 31: Royal Cdn Legion Awards application deadline<br>• May 31: Dr. David Clarke Bursary awarded<br>• Aug 15: Provincial Scholarships & Bursaries are issued; based on Standard Ministry Scores (SMS)<br>• Sep 1: Get Provincial Scholarship validated at university being attended |
| **High School Courses** (MBSS) | Dec 5/98 | • Dec 5: Start preparing for the January Provincial Exams<br>• Jan 10: Write Provincial Exams (need to have photo ID & know your PEN (Personal Education Number))<br>• May 1: Start preparing for the June Provincial Exams<br>• Jun 1: Write Provincial Exams |
| **University of Alberta** (Edmonton, Alberta) | Dec 5/98 | • Dec 5: Have we heard from U of A re: *Academic Excellence* program?<br>• Feb 8: Submit entrance application to U of Alberta; conditional acceptances granted approx end of next January<br>• Mar 1: *Scholastic Distinction Award* applications due (nominated by high school)<br>• Mar 15: Entrance Leadership Scholarship applications deadline<br>• May 1: Begin registering for courses<br>• May 1: Entrance applications are due (all are considered for the "Entrance Academic Scholarships" with application)<br>• May 5: *Scholastic Distinction Award* are issued<br>• May 30: *Entrance Academic Scholarships* are awarded<br>• Aug 1: Deadline for receipt of transcripts<br>• Sep 30: *Entrance Academic Scholarships* are awarded |

| Component | Date | Actions & Deadlines |
|---|---|---|
| **Queens University** (Kingston, Ontario) | Dec 15/98 | • Dec 15: Submit application form to Ontario for Queen's<br>• Apr 30: Entrance Bursaries application deadline<br>• May 15: Entrance admission confirmations are mailed out by today<br>• May 25: Must apply to Residence by today c/w $500.00 deposit (guaranteed a space only until June 1). $300.00 is refundable if space is cancelled before July 9.<br>• Jun 01: Deadline to confirm acceptance of advanced admission & registration for residence.<br>• Jul 10: Entrance Bursaries awarded<br>• Aug 15: Deadline for receipt of transcripts |
| **McGill University** (Montréal, Québec) | Jan 10/99 | • Jan 10: Scholarship application prepared (review electronic application first)<br>• Feb 24: Entrance application deadline (early admission)<br>• May 1: Confirmation due from McGill re: entrance & scholarships<br>• Jun 1: Deadline to confirm acceptance of advanced admission & registration for residence. |
| **Financing** | May 2/99 | • May 2: Begin looking into student loans (see pg 24 of 98/99 *Student Guidebook for Graduates* from MBSS)<br>• Jun 4: Send in applications for financial assistance; student loans (see pg 24 of *Student Guidebook for Graduates* from MBSS). Deadline is June 30. |

March and April of Christy's Grade 12 year was a fun time. Responses came back from the five schools—she received early admission to all of them. This led us into the third stage of the project.

*Choose one school and prepare to attend (late in Grade 12):*

Having received early admission to five excellent schools, the time came for Christy to pick the one school she wanted to attend. Late in April of her Grade 12 year, she chose to attend McGill University in Montréal, Québec. Now our sole focus was to prepare for her to attend McGill in the fall. It also meant we had to notify the other schools about her decision. Our Projecteze Table evolved again as I deleted the information for the other schools and expanded the level of detail and key dates for McGill University. I updated the table in early May, as shown below. Together, Christy and I walked through all of the dates and tasks. In August of that year, Christy flew 3,000 miles to begin her first year at McGill.

From March through June of her senior year in high school, Christy also applied for several scholarships and received three awards that helped finance her first year of post-secondary education.

| Component | Date | Actions & Deadlines |
|---|---|---|
| University Applications | May 1/99 | • May 1: Fill out *Post-Secondary Institution Choices* Form at school to state where you want to have final transcripts sent in early August.<br>• May 5: The government issues Transcript Verification Report (TVR) to schools in early May confirming graduation requirements; review to confirm it is accurate.<br>• Jul 6: Write to all references to tell them how you are making out (school chosen, etc.) |
| Scholarships | May 1/99 | • May 1: Check with the Career Preparation Counselors to see if you qualify as a candidate for a Provincial or District scholarship<br>• May 31: Royal Cdn Legion Awards application deadline<br>• May 31: Dr. David Clarke Bursary awarded |
| High School Courses (MBSS) | May 1/99 | • May 1: Start preparing for the June Provincial Exams<br>• Jun 1: Write Provincial Exams |
| Financing | May 2/99 | • May 2: Begin looking into student loans (see pg 24 of 98/99 *Student Guidebook for Graduates* from MBSS)<br>• Jun 4: Send in applications for financial assistance; student loans (see pg 24 of 98/99 Student Guidebook for Graduates from MBSS)<br>• Jun 30: Suggested date by which student loan applications should be submitted to the Ministry of Education, Skills & Training (Student Assistance Program). |
| McGill University (Montréal, Québec) | May 2/99 | • May 2: Write letters declining acceptance at other schools<br>• May 3: Respond with confirmation of acceptance c/w photocopies confirming Cdn citizenship (required by June 1)<br>• May 5: Prepare a budget for attending McGill<br>• May 5: Begin studying the specific course options and identify preferences<br>• May 16: Complete Housing application with Christy and send by courier c/w $675.50<br>• May 25: Deadline to apply to Residence by today c/w $500.00 deposit (guaranteed a space only until June 1). $300.00 is refundable if space is cancelled before July 9.<br>• Jun 1: Deadline to confirm acceptance of advanced admission & registration for residence.<br>• Jun 9: Establish a preliminary course schedule; package is coming by June 3.<br>• Jun 10: Confirm what needs to be done re: medical coverage for Christy while in Québec.<br>• Jun 15: Received tuition fee confirmation; $200.00 deposit sent on April 25<br>• Jul 2: Arrange Christy's flights to/from Montréal<br>• Jul 3: Read through *Freshman Handbook* and set up course schedule.<br>• Jul 15: Call Registrar's office to check that:<br>1) File is complete and that transcripts will be forthcoming. (transcripts are not due out until July 30; will check back in early August).<br>2) Have the signed scholarship forms been sent in to COBSS yet?<br>• Jul 15: Make a list of what Christy needs to take [bedding, clothing, etc.]<br>• Jul 20: Order computer (iMac) & printer at McGill Computer Store.<br>• Aug 3: Check with Registrar that transcripts have been received. Are the COBSS scholarship funds in yet? |

| Component | Date | Actions & Deadlines |
|---|---|---|
| | | • Aug 4: Confirm courses registration and fit of schedule via MARS; first available to Christy between 6:00 am - 10:00 pm, Aug 4.<br>• Aug 16: Arrange to get copy of high school transcripts (copy required for Advising Session on Aug 25)<br>• Aug 23: Residence possession date; McGill notified of late arrival<br>• Aug 23: 8:05 pm, (AC flight 1608)—Christy leaves for Montréal; must have at least two pieces of ID, one w/photo.<br>• Aug 24: Check into Residence (between 9:00 am - 9:00 pm, Bishop Mountain Hall)<br>• Aug 24: Pick up student ID card at Room 232, Stephen Leacock Bldg (need two pieces of personal ID).<br>• Aug 24: Open a bank account on campus & get a safety deposit box for return airplane tickets.<br>• Aug 25: Advising Session (2:30 pm, Room W120, Arts Building)<br>• Aug 26: Tour campus and become familiar with all facilities, including computer facilities.<br>• Aug 27: Attend the University Orientation session (9:30 - 10:00 am, Room 132, Fieldhouse Auditorium, Stephen Leacock Building); take copy of transcript & other documents needed per *Freshman Handbook.*<br>• Aug 27: Change your mailing address and contact information on SATURN<br>• Sep 1: Classes begin<br>• Sep 8: Decide if you want to make any changes to the courses you are registered in. (if so, the changes must be authorized by a Freshman Advisor in Room 110, Arts Building).<br>• Sep 20: Contact Student Affairs Office (open 10:00 am - 4:00 pm, 853 Sherbrooke Street; Tel: 398-4210) about attending the free non-credit mini-course in October called "University Success". This course covers skills in studying & learning at university.<br>• Sep 24: Deadline for tuition payment<br>• Dec 21: Last day of exams (fly home)<br>• Dec 22: Christy flies home (Arrives 3:10 pm; flight 1615)<br>• Jan 4: Classes resume<br>• Jan 4: 6:50 AM: Christy leaves for Montréal.<br>• Apr 28: Last day of exams (fly home)<br>• Apr 29: Christy flies home (Arrives 12:54 PM; flight 258)<br>• May 1: Book all flights for Christy's next school year |

Christy completed a Bachelor of Science degree at McGill University in four years. She has since completed a Masters degree at the University of Calgary.

Laurence Seton © | Projecteze Inc.

## Starting University Classes

*The difference between school and life?*
*In school, you're taught a lesson and then given a test.*
*In life, you're given a test that teaches you a lesson.*
—Tom Bodett

Similar to my own experience in university, Christy was immediately inundated with homework and assignments. In her first week, the instructors handed out course outlines, dates for midterm and final exams, and assignments that would have to be completed by the following week. Succeeding in this environment demands a good organizational system.

The following is an example of a Projecteze Table for a university student early in the first year. Creating a row for each course as well as for other extra-curricular activities makes it easy to stay ahead of the wave and be more fully prepared for completing assignments and writing exams.

In this chapter I've illustrated how students will benefit from using my Projecteze method to stay abreast of all the demands, assignments, and requirements in high school and post-secondary environments. It's not difficult to understand how teachers—at every level—can use Projecteze to organize and manage the extreme challenges that are part of their profession. Advanced learning requires advanced organization—this results in advanced opportunities for academic excellence.

| Subject | Date | Prty | Homework, Exams & Other |
|---------|------|------|-------------------------|
| Vehicle | Sept 7 | 1 | • Sept 7: Get onto waiting list for parking spot; estimated at 6 months wait. $100 deposit required.<br>• Confirm best bus route and times<br>• Get new winter tires onto car<br>• Oct 15: Renew car insurance |
| Bookstore | Sept 8 | 1 | • Texts to buy:<br>- Basic Introductory Chemistry ($115.00)<br>- Lives of Famous Romans ($38.00)<br>- Essential Physics ($105.00)<br>- Geological Foundations ($90.00)<br>- Sociology ($95.00)<br><br>• Other supplies to pick up:<br>- notepads, pens, highlighters,<br>- lab supplies for Chem |
| Chemistry 201 | Sept 8 | 1 | • Sept 8: Read chapter 1 & complete first exercise in workbook, before next class<br>• Sept 15: Assignment #1 due<br>• Oct 12: 1st mid-term exam<br>• Nov 13: 2nd mid-term exam<br>• Dec 13: Final exam |
| Geology 201 | Sept 8 | 2 | • Sept 8: Reading & assignment #1; due Sept 14<br>• Oct 18: Mid-term exam<br>• Dec 6: Final exam |
| Physics 221 | Sept 9 | 1 | • Sept 9: Read chapters 1 & 2, and complete chapter quizzes; due Sept 13<br>• Sept 16: Lab this week has been cancelled<br>• Oct 19: Mid-term exam<br>• Dec 8: Final exam |
| Recreation | Sept 9 | 3 | • Sign up for an intramural hockey team; $150.00 deposit required<br>• Get locker at Phys Ed building<br>• Bring gear to school<br>• Join the Ski Club |
| Greek & Roman Studies 205 | Sept 11 | 2 | • Weekend: Reading *Lives of Famous Romans* (by Sept 24)<br>• Oct 21: Mid-term paper due<br>• Nov 30: Final paper due |
| Sociology 201 | Sept 11 | 2 | • Weekend: Read chapters 1 & 2<br>• Sept 20: Paper due on rationale behind social institutions<br>• Oct 21: Mid-term exam<br>• Dec 10: Final exam |
| Registrar | Sept 20 | 1 | • Look into changing Biology course for the 2nd semester; deadline is Nov 10 |
| Financial | Sept 21 | 1 | • Sept 21: Pay tuition for 1st semester – deadline is Sept 24<br>• Sept 22: Submit confirmation of attendance & tuition payment, for release of student loans |

# Projecteze For Teams:
# Organization-wide Benefits

*We make a living by what we get,*
*but we make a life by what we give.*
–Winston Churchill

Once you've started using the Projecteze system and realize how much being on top of everything benefits you, the next step is to use the Projecteze system for group initiatives. Projecteze can be applied to help teams and organizations manage projects with the same ease and efficiency that individuals achieve.

Team Projecteze Table

Previous versions of MS Word would not allow a document to be worked on simultaneously by more than one person at a time but the release of MS Word 2010 (for the PC) and 2011 (for the Mac) has changed all that. These versions of MS Office include a feature called "Live Collaboration Functions" which allows many people to work on documents at the same time, over a network or over the internet.

Imagine you've been thrown into a new initiative that collectively involves people from different areas within your company or organization who are tasked with accomplishing a common defined objective. In the same way that you created a Projecteze Table for yourself, the team can create and share a common Team Projecteze Table.

The collaboration feature in MS Word takes the concept and power of a Team Projecteze Table to new heights. Float a copy of a Team Projecteze Table on any network server, or the internet, where it can be accessed by everyone on the team, add password protection (sharing it with all the team members), and let the group work from that common table. Team members can make changes and updates as they occur, providing everyone on the team with a current status of commitments and action items being tracked by the group.

In this way, MS Word provides multiple users with a real-time presence, paragraph by paragraph, in co-authored documents. When you access a common Team Projecteze Table, you will see where other authors are editing as they edit, and they will see where you are editing as you edit. You don't need to press a button to let others know where you are; Word keeps everyone's presence in sync in real-time automatically. Teammates can make real-time changes to a shared Team Projecteze Table without ever leaving the Word application.

This concept becomes even more powerful when it's applied internationally for project teams who are spread around the globe and are working on a common project but at different times. Using cloud computing on the internet and a Team Projecteze Table will enable everyone on the team to tap into the table, find out what the most current status is and make updates for the rest of the team to see – as they complete action items that other team members are dependent on.

Now, I'll be the first to acknowledge there are numerous other applications out there that will provide team coordination capabilities but, as I described in Chapter One, they will invariable require buying specialized software, will involve a substantial learning curve and will be more complicated than using the simple, easy, already available table capabilities found right in MS Word.

Using the Projecteze system corporately will increase a team's efficiency and productivity–giving the organization an edge on being more competitive in the marketplace. While Projecteze can have a very direct and positive effect on the corporate bottom line, the non-monetary rewards are perhaps even more substantial.

Decades of human resource studies have shown that a sense of personal accomplishment and other less quantifiable benefits usually appeal to us more than monetary rewards. People are motivated by the feelings associated with successfully completing objectives and performing well.

When corporations implement the Projecteze system throughout their organization, they are helping everyone in it to succeed individually and as a team. With Projecteze, employees develop a greater sense of trust with each other–from knowing that the commitments and actions they are relying on won't be forgotten but will instead be addressed, thereby enabling every-one to perform at a higher level. It becomes a self-fulfilling cycle that grows and benefits both the corporation and everyone involved.

### *Conclusion*
# The Ultimate Benefit

*Your entire life journey
ultimately consists of the step
you are taking at this moment
so give it your fullest attention.*
−Eckhart Tolle

This book introduced you to an organizational system that is both simple and sophisticated. You learned how to build your own Projecteze Table and capture just the right level of detail that you need to always be one step ahead on all your projects—in the workplace, at home and at school. You learned that the Projecteze system enables you to be more effective and always prepared for dealing with whatever comes your way.

Projecteze provides a functionality and flexibility not found in other systems. It is an easy to use tool for proactively managing all the day-to-day responsibilities that are aimed directly at you. In a matter of only minutes each day, you can stay ahead of the key commitments and action items from all of your projects and know where you should be focusing your attention.

Used diligently, Projecteze will allow you to interact with the world more spontaneously and in the moment. By clearing the mental clutter, Projecteze lets you think about and focus on one responsibility or commitment at a time. This system helps you to be more present so you can have stronger relationships which is a foundational aspect of experiencing personal satisfaction and success in any environment.

I invite you to use Projecteze for at least one month. Stick with it and use it every day at work. And if you stop using it, get back to it. Your health will thank you. You'll benefit from reduced stress levels and Projecteze will help to keep those stress levels in check, day after day.

You will come to enjoy benefits that transcend the system itself as well. Having key project information presented this way helps issues gel into patterns that cross many projects. Whether you use Projecteze as an individual or as a team member, you will experience greater awareness and enhanced insight in everything you do because you will be able to step back and see the bigger picture.

You should expect to recognize new ideas and solutions that you might have otherwise missed if you were to have considered each issue or project in isolation. This system lets you approach the world with fresh eyes, to become aware of new questions and new solutions. It allows you to more freely tap into your intuition and creativity.

A Projecteze Table is a very powerful tool for helping you balance all aspects of your life. The degree to which you can increase your personal space and availability will have a great bearing on your success in all areas—professional, mental, emotional, physical, social and spiritual. They are all tied together in the realm of personal well being. Define and honour your personal boundaries. Learn to step away from the chaos. Experience the feeling of being in control so you can relax, and take more time for yourself and your relationships.

The ultimate benefit from using the Projecteze system is that it can give you back yourself. Projecteze will help you to be more aware of where it is you need and want to spend your time and it will provide you with the support system necessary to follow through on that awareness. This can be a very powerful and enjoyable process. It has been for me.

I have achieved the life I vowed to live when I was a teenager. My wife and I have been married for over 35 years. We have both dedicated ourselves to and been a big part of the lives of our two children. It is a source of tremendous pride to have been able to work with my daughter and help her achieve her academic and professional goals. It was extremely rewarding and enjoyable to have been there for my son and coach him in hockey for ten years. I made sure I had time for my family and the Projecteze system was instrumental in my ability to succeed on all fronts—at work and at home.

Having worked in business for over 30 years, I have come to appreciate just how important relationships are and I really appreciate the relationships I have with my family, friends, co-workers and clients. Inevitably, the most rewarding experiences in life will involve an interaction with someone else. Projecteze can help you stay on top of everything so you can be more present and available for the people that matter to you.

I sincerely hope you use the Projecteze system to help you live the life you desire. My wish for you is to also have the personal freedom and connection that Projecteze has brought to me and my family. You deserve it and so do the people in your life.

## Courses on the Projecteze System

*An investment in knowledge always pays the best interest.*
–Benjamin Franklin

Do you want to:

- Achieve the success you are striving for without sacrificing your life in the process?

- Experience the enjoyment of having more time for yourself and your family?

- Learn the difference between having a "full life" and a "fulfilling life"?

There are many dimensions to the Projecteze system. So many, in fact, that we've developed courses to help you and your employees through the process.

We help people learn the Projecteze system quickly, to gain a deeper understanding of how to fully harness its capabilities for their own specific situation.

Our courses can help you, your team and your organization learn how to maximize your effectiveness, strengthen relationships, and experience greater personal satisfaction from a job well done.

To learn more about our courses, go to the website www.OnTopOfEverything.com.

## Share Your Projecteze Experiences

In the interest of enhancing the usefulness of the Projecteze system for all, I encourage you to share your creative new ideas of how you've used the system. Tell the rest of us how you've harnessed the flexibility of the Projecteze system.

* Where and how have you used the Projecteze system to improve your own efficiency and effectiveness?

* What innovations or creative applications have resulted in "Aha!" experiences for you?

* What are some of the applications you've found for the Projecteze system and what were the benefits you gained?

There is no end to where the adaptability of this system can be applied. Together we can build a pool of ideas for applying the system to its maximum—for everyone's benefit. By sharing our own experiences and successes with the Projecteze system, we can all benefit.

Share your ideas and experiences at the website www.OnTopOfEverything.com.

As you use the Projecteze system and see how well it works, spread the word and tell your friends and co-workers about it. The more we help others succeed, the more we help ourselves succeed. Remember, we're all in this together!

## Bibliography

Allen, David. *Getting Things Done: The art of stress-free productivity*. New York: Penguin Group, 2001.

Babauta, Leo. *Zen To Done: The ultimate simple productivity system*. CreateSpace, 2008.

Babauta, Leo. *The Power of Less: The fine art of limiting yourself to the essential...in business and in life*. New York: Hyperion, 2009.

Crowe, Andy. *Alpha Project Managers: What the top 2% know that everyone else does not*. Velociteach Press, 2006

Covey, Stephen, A. Roger Merrill, and Rebecca R. Merrill. *First Things First*. New York: Simon & Shuster, 1994.

Jensen, Bill. *Simplicity: The new competitive advantage*. Basic Books, 2001.

Lesser, Marc. *Less: Accomplishing more by doing less*. Novato, California: New World Library, 2009.

Medina, John. *Brain Rules: 12 principles for surviving and thriving at work, home, and school*. Seattle: Pear Press, 2008.

Tolle, Eckhart. *The Power of Now: A guide to spiritual enlightenment*. Novato, California: New World Library, 1999.

Tolle, Eckhart. *A New Earth: Awakening to your life's purpose*. New York: Penguin Group, 2005.

# Appendices

## Appendix A

## MS Word Conversion Tables For Projecteze Procedures

## Commands by Projecteze Procedure:

| Setting up a shortcut keystroke for bullets: | |
|---|---|
| MS Word 2003 (PC) | *Insert>Symbol>Symbol tab>Font.* Set *Character code* to *183.* The *from* box beside this should show *Symbol (decimal).* Click the *Shortcut Key* button, click into the box *Press new shortcut key,* hold "Ctrl + 0" (holding the Ctrl key down as you push the zero key); then release both keys. Hit the *Assign* button. *OK>Close* |
| MS Word 2004 (Mac) | *Insert>Symbol>Symbols* tab>set font to *Symbol>*select "bullet" (confirm it is character 183). *Shortcut Key>Press new shortcut key>*hold "Ctrl + 0">*Assign>OK>Close* |
| MS Word 2007 & 2010 (PC) | *Insert Ribbon>Symbol* Icon>*More Symbols>Symbols* tab>set font to *Symbol.* Set *Character code* to 183. *Shortcut Key>Press new shortcut key>* hold "Ctrl + 0"> *Assign>OK>Close* |
| MS Word 2011 (Mac) | *Insert>Symbol>Advanced Symbol> Symbols* tab>set font to *Symbol>*select "bullet" (confirm it is character 183). *Keyboard Shortcut>Press new shortcut key>*hold "Ctrl + 0">*Assign>OK>Close* |

| Sorting the Table: (With your cursor anywhere inside the table) | |
|---|---|
| MS Word 2003 (PC) & 2004 (Mac) | *Table>Sort.* Choose Sort by *Date* and *Prty* (both Ascending)>*OK* |
| MS Word 2007 & 2010 (PC) | *Home Ribbon>Sort* Icon <u>or</u> *Table Tools>Layout Ribbon>Data Group>Sort* Icon. Sort box opens. Choose Sort by *Date* and *Prty* (both Ascending)>*OK* |
| MS Word 2011 (Mac) | *Home Ribbon>Sort* Icon <u>or</u> *Table Layout Ribbon>Data Group>Sort* Icon. Sort box opens. Choose Sort by *Date* and *Prty* (both Ascending)>*OK* |

| Saving With A Password: | |
|---|---|
| MS Word 2003 (PC) | *File>Save As>Tools button>Security Options>Password to Open* |
| MS Word 2004 (Mac) | *File>Save As>Options> Password to Open* |
| MS Word 2007 (PC) | *MS Office Button>Prepare>Encrypt Document>Encrypt With Password* |
| MS Word 2010 (PC) | *File>Info>Permissions>Protect Document>Encrypt with Password* |
| MS Word 2011 (Mac) | *Word>Preferences>Personal Settings>Security>Password to Open* |

| Applying Existing Formatting To Pasted Text: | |
|---|---|
| All versions of MS Word | Copy text from any source. Then use *Edit>Paste Special>Unformatted Text.* This will cause the formatting of the newly pasted text to match the existing formatting in the Projecteze Table. Alternatively, use the *Format Painter.* |

# Commands by version of MS Word:

| MS Word 2003 (PC) | |
|---|---|
| Saving With A Password | *File>Save As>Tools button>Security Options>Password to Open* |
| Sorting the Table | With your cursor anywhere inside the table, *Table>Sort*. Choose Sort by *Date* and *Prty* (both Ascending)>*OK* |
| Bullets shortcut keystroke | *Insert>Symbol>Symbol tab>Font*. Set *Character code* to *183*. The *from* box beside this should show *Symbol (decimal)*. Click the *Shortcut Key* button, click into the box *Press new shortcut key*, hold "Ctrl + 0" (holding the Ctrl key down as you push the zero key); then release both keys. Hit the *Assign* button. *OK>Close* |

| MS Word 2004 (Mac) | |
|---|---|
| Saving With A Password | *File>Save As>Options> Password to Open* |
| Sorting the Table | With your cursor anywhere inside the table, *Table>Sort*. Choose Sort by *Date* and *Prty* (both Ascending)>*OK* |
| Bullets shortcut keystroke | *Insert>Symbol>Symbols tab>*set font to *Symbol>*select "bullet" (confirm it is character 183). *Shortcut Key>Press new shortcut key>*hold "Ctrl + 0">*Assign>OK>Close* |

| MS Word 2007 (PC) | |
|---|---|
| Saving With A Password | *MS Office Button>Prepare>Encrypt Document>Encrypt With Password* |
| Sorting the Table | With your cursor anywhere inside the table, use either:<br>1.  *Home Ribbon>Sort* Icon. Sort box opens. or<br>2.  *Table Tools>Layout Ribbon>Data Group>Sort* Icon. Sort box opens.<br>Choose Sort by *Date* and *Prty* (both Ascending)>*OK* |
| Bullets shortcut keystroke | *Insert Ribbon>Symbol* Icon*>More Symbols>Symbols tab>*set font to *Symbol*. Set *Character code* to *183*. *Shortcut Key>Press new shortcut key>* hold "Ctrl + 0">*Assign>OK>Close* |

| MS Word 2010 (PC) | |
|---|---|
| Saving With A Password | *File>Info>Permissions>Protect Document>Encrypt with Password* |
| Sorting the Table | With your cursor anywhere inside the table, use either:<br>1)  *Home Ribbon>Sort* Icon. Sort box opens. or<br>2)  *Table Tools>Layout Ribbon>Data Group>Sort* Icon. Sort box opens.<br>Choose Sort by *Date* and *Prty* (both Ascending)>*OK* |
| Bullets shortcut keystroke | *Insert Ribbon>Symbol* Icon*>More Symbols>Symbols tab>*set font to *Symbol*. Set *Character code* to *183*. *Shortcut Key>Press new shortcut key>* hold "Ctrl + 0">*Assign>OK>Close* |

| MS Word 2011 (Mac) | |
|---|---|
| Saving With A Password | *Word>Preferences>Personal Settings>Security>Password to Open* |
| Sorting the Table | With your cursor anywhere inside the table, use either:<br>1)  *Home Ribbon>Sort* Icon. Sort box opens. or<br>2)  *Table Layout Ribbon>Data Group>Sort* Icon. Sort box opens.<br>Choose Sort by *Date* and *Prty* (both Ascending)>*OK* |
| Bullets shortcut keystroke | *Insert>Symbol>Advanced Symbol> Symbols tab>*set font to *Symbol>*select "bullet" (confirm it is character 183). *Keyboard Shortcut>Press new shortcut key>*hold "Ctrl + 0">*Assign>OK>Close* |

## *Appendix B*

Quick Steps To Set Up A Blank Projecteze Table

If you did not download a pre-formatted blank Projecteze Table from the website, you can follow these steps to set up your own blank Projecteze Table:

a) Use a standard letter size (8.5" x 11") page with portrait orientation.

b) Set the page margins to be 0.5" on the left and right side for the entire document.

c) At the top of the first page, type "Projecteze: *Your Name*". Center this text and set the font size at 12 point and make it bold.

d) Drop down one line, using <Return>, pull down the *Table Menu* and select *Insert Table*. Follow the directions to create a table with **four columns** and **seven rows**.

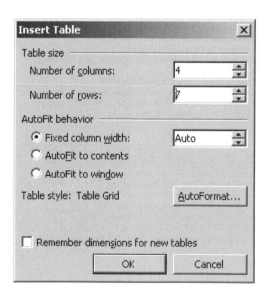

Laurence Seton © | Projecteze Inc.

e) Select the entire table and set the font to Times New Roman, 10 point.

f) Select the entire table again, and use menus *Table>Properties>Row* tab to make sure there is a check beside *Allow row to break across pages*. Then select *Table* tab, *Centre*.

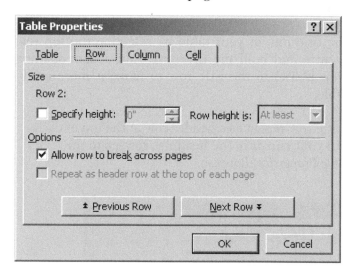

g) Set the overall table width using *Table>Table Properties> Table* tab, *Preferred width*, set to 7.5". Then go to the *Column* tab to set the four column widths (left to right) to: 1.24", 0.61", 0.42" and 5.23" (for a total width of 7.5").

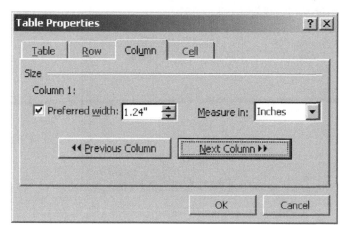

h) Type the following headings into the top row of the four columns in your table:

- Project
- Date
- Prty [short for "Priority']
- Commitments & Action Items

i) Format the title row in your table by selecting the top row only, then centre and bold the title text. Add a light shading (such as Grey 12.5%) to the title row to make it more easily distinguishable.

j) Have the title row repeat as a header row at the top of each page. With your cursor in the headings row, go to the *Table>Table Properties>Row* tab.

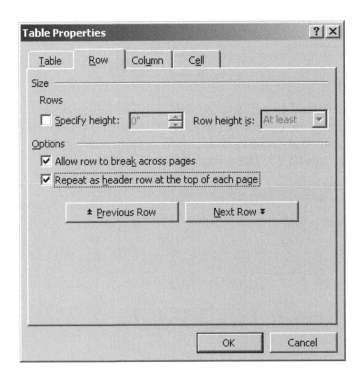

Laurence Seton © | Projecteze Inc.

Your table should now look like this:

| Project | Date | Prty | Commitments & Action Items |
|---------|------|------|----------------------------|
|         |      |      |                            |
|         |      |      |                            |
|         |      |      |                            |
|         |      |      |                            |
|         |      |      |                            |
|         |      |      |                            |

k) Now set the alignment for the rows below the header row to:

- Left justified: Project, Commitments & Actions Items columns.
- Centered: Date, Prty columns.

l) Add bolding to the entire Project column.

## *Appendix C*

Detailed Instructions
For Setting Up, Formatting And
Using The Projecteze Table


These detailed step-by-step instructions for setting up a Projecteze Table refer to the program menus found in MS Word 2003. If you are using a more recent version of MS Word, please see the conversion tables in Appendices A and D as well.

**Name and save your document:**

1) Open a new page in Microsoft Word

2) Save this document to the folder you want to place it in. Go to the menus *File>Save As*, go to the folder you want to place it in or you can create a new folder using the *Create New Folder* icon. Type the name *Your name-yyyy-mm-dd* into the *File name* box (where the *yyyy*, *mm* and *dd* represent *year, month and date*). Click the *Save* button.

**Password protecting your Projecteze Table:**

3) Go to *File>Save As>Tools button>Security Options>Password to Open*
[Mac®: *File>Save As> Options> Password to Open*]

4) With the cursor in the top blank field, enter your password, click *OK*. Be sure to remember your password.

5) Click on *Save*. Tell it to replace existing file, if it asks you.

**Set the page margins:**

6) On the *File* menu, click *Page Setup*, and then click the *Margins* tab. [Mac®: *File>Page Setup*, from Settings select *Microsoft Word* and then click the *Margins* tab]

7) Set Right and Left to 0.5", set Top and Bottom to 0.7".

8) Click on *OK*.

**Putting your name on the document:**

9) With your cursor in the top of the first page, type in "Projecteze: *Your Name*"

10) Highlight this text with the cursor and format it using *Format>Font>Font* to Times New Roman, *Font Style* to Bold, *Size* to 12; then click on *OK*

11) With your cursor in this same row that you just typed, centre the text by using *Format> Paragraph>Indents and Spacing tab>General Alignment*. [Mac®: *Format> Paragraph>Indents and Spacing tab>Alignment*] Set it to *Centre* [Mac®: *Centered*] and click *OK*

**Insert your Projecteze Table:**

12) Hit your *Enter* key to drop down one more row

13) From the menus, choose *Table>Insert>Table*.

14) Enter 4 columns and 7 rows

15) Click on *OK*

*Alternatively, you can create a table in another very simple way:*

a.  Type a "+" sign where you want the table to start

b.  Tab three times

c.  Type a "+" sign

d.  Repeat steps b and c for each column (four columns in total)

e.  Hit Enter

f.  This creates a table with one row. To add more rows, put your cursor in the bottom right cell of the table and hit Tab. Continue to do this for every additional row you require.

**Format the font for entire table:**

16) *Table>Select>Table*

17) *Format>Font>Font tab*

18) Choose *Times New Roman* as the Font, *Regular* as the Font Style and *10* as the Size [This font and size is used because it uses less space and is easy to read.]

19) Click on *OK*

**Format the columns in the table:**

20) Put your cursor in the top row, first column of your table

21) Choose *Table>Select>Column*

22) *Format>Paragraph>Indents and Spacing> Alignment>Left*

23) Click on *OK*

24) *Format>Font>Font tab*, select *Bold*

25) Click on *OK*

26) Put your cursor in the top row, second column of the table

27) *Table>Select>Column*

28) *Format>Paragraph>Indents and Spacing>Alignment>Centered*

29) Click on *OK*

Laurence Seton © | Projecteze Inc.

30) Put your cursor in the top row, third column of the table

31) *Table>Select>Column*

32) *Format>Paragraph>Indents and Spacing>Alignment>Centered*

33) Click on *OK*

34) Put your cursor in the top row, fourth column of the table

35) *Table>Select>Column*

36) *Format>Paragraph>Indents and Spacing> Alignment>Left*

37) Click on *OK*

**Setting table properties:**

38) *Table>Select>Table*

39) *Table>Table Properties>Table tab>Preferred Width* to 7.50"
and *Alignment* to Centre

40) *Table>Table Properties>Row>Options.* Put a check beside
*Allow row to break across pages*

41) *Table>Table Properties>Column tab.* Type in the following
column widths, hitting the *Next Column* button after
each entry:
Column 1: 1.24"
Column 2: 0.61"
Column 3: 0.42"
Column 4: 5.23"

42) *Table>Table Properties>Cell tab>Vertical alignment* to *Top*

43) Click on *OK*

44) *File>Save*

An alternate way to access *Table Properties* is to right mouse-click the four-headed arrow that appears when you hold you mouse outside the top left corner or bottom right corner of the table. Select *Table Properties* from the drop down list that shows up.

You can also re-size the entire table by grabbing the box at the bottom right hand corner of the table that shows up when you hold your mouse over the table. Pull the box down to make the table larger or up to make the table smaller. You can make the table narrower by dragging the mouse to the centre of the table or wider by moving it away from the centre.

**Format the top (title) row in the table:**

45) With the cursor anywhere in the top row, select
*Table>Select>Row*

46) *Format>Font>Font tab*, select *Bold*

47) *Format>Borders & Shading>Shading tab>Fill* to a light grey (Grey-12.5% or the colour of your choosing)

48) Click on *OK*

49) *Table>Table Properties>Cell tab*. Put a check beside *Repeat as header row at the top of each page*

50) Click on *OK*

51) *Format>Paragraph>Indents and Spacing> General - Alignment*. Set to *Centered* - to centre align the table titles row

52) Click on *OK*

You should now be able to enter the following descriptions into the title row, one for each column:
Project, Date, Prty, Commitments & Action Items.
[Prty is short for Priority]

**Setting an indent for the Commitments & Action Items column:**

53) With your cursor still in the fourth column,
select *Table>Select>Column*

54) *Format>Paragraph>Indentation>Special*
[Mac®: *Format>Paragraph>Indents & Spacing>
Indentation>Special*]. Set to *Hanging by 0.1"*

**Setting up a shortcut keystroke for inserting bullets:**

55) With the cursor flashing anywhere on the page, select
*Insert>Symbol>Symbol tab>Font*. Set *Character code* to *183*.
The *from* box beside this should show *Symbol (decimal)*

56) Click the *Shortcut Key* button, click into the box
(also called a field) *Press new shortcut key*, hold "Ctrl + 0"
(holding the Ctrl key down as you push the zero key);
then release the keys

57) Hit the *Assign* button

58) Click on *OK*

59) Click on *Close*
You can now use the combination of *Ctrl+0* at any time
to enter this type of bullet which will be very helpful
for identifying individual packets of information
in your Projecteze Table.
[Alternatively, *Option+8* can be used to create
a similar type of bullet on the Mac.]

**Setting up the page header:**

60) *View>Header and Footer*. Type "Page" and a space in the header

61) Click the first icon in the header/footer toolbar that just showed up (*Insert Page Number*). Type another space, type "of", type another space, and click the second icon in the header/footer toolbar (*Insert Number of Pages*)

62) While still in the header and following what you just typed in, hit the "Tab" key twice and type "Confidential!"

63) Again, hit the "Tab" key twice and click the fourth icon in the header/footer toolbar (*Insert Date*)

64) Choose the *Close* icon at the right end of the header/footer toolbar. The date field you just entered will automatically update each day when you open your Projecteze Table.

65) If you would like the date to show up in a different format (e.g. mmm dd/yy), you can change it. Select *View>Header and Footer*. Click onto the date in the header, right mouse click it, choose *Edit Field*, select the formatting you would like and hit *OK*. Then click *Close* on the header/footer toolbar.

[If the format you want isn't showing, you can type it into the field right under *Date formats* using m for the month, d for the day and y for the year, Example: mmm dd/yy gives you Sep 15/10.]

[Mac: The steps to accomplish this on the Mac are, for a change, somewhat more extensive.
Use:
*View>Header and Footer*
Place your cursor in the right hand side of the header (after tabbing across from "Confidential!")
*Insert>Field*
*Categories:>Date and Time*

*Field Name>Date*
*Options* button
Select date format preferred
Click the *Add to Field* button
Click *OK*
Click *OK*]

**Filling In Your Projecteze Table:**

66) Enter information into the first blank row of the table, under the table title row, in the following manner:

a.  First column: Enter the name of one of your projects

b.  Second column: Enter the next date you will have to take action on this project, as "mmm dd" or "mmm dd/yy"

c.  Third column: Enter the priority you would assign to this action item, between 1 and 5

d.  Fourth column: Insert a bullet (*Cntl+0*), a space, and enter a next action date, colon, a description of the item you will have to take action on next for that project, (the date the commitment was made, in brackets).

Using this methodology, continue to populate your new Projecteze Table. Be sure to save it every so often to ensure the valuable information you are entering doesn't get lost.

A representative example of how the table should look is shown below:

| Project | Date | Prty | Commitments & Action Items |
|---------|------|------|----------------------------|
| Project 1 | Mar 6 | 2 | • Mar 6: A basic description of the commitment or action item to be tracked (date commitment was made) |
| | | | |
| | | | |
| | | | |

## Sorting Your Projecteze Table

67) With your cursor anywhere inside your Projecteze Table and it blinking (i.e. not highlighting text in which case it will not be flashing), select *Table>Sort*. The Sort window will open for you.

68) Using the drop down menus (arrows pointing downward), choose *Sort by: Date* and *Then by: Prty. Ascending* should be selected already for both of these. *My list has: header row* should also be selected already at the bottom of the sort window.

69) Click *OK*.

This will re-sort your Projecteze Table—firstly by the date and then by the priority you have assigned to each row.

Remember that as you continue to work with and update the information in your table, you can and should re-sort it repeatedly to bring the next most pressing action items and highest priorities to the top of your table and the forefront of your attention.

## Appendix D

MS Word 2003 to 2007 Menus

Conversions Table

The following table provides a conversion for menus (commands) found in MS Word 2003 versus MS 2007.

| Word 2003 Location | Word 2007 Location | Keyboard Shortcut |
|---|---|---|
| **"File" Menu:** | | |
| File > New | Office Button > New | Ctrl-N |
| File > Open | Office Button > Open | Ctrl-O |
| File > Close | Office Button > Close | Ctrl-W |
| File > Save | Office Button > Save *or* Quick Access toolbar > Save icon | Ctrl-S |
| File > Save As | Office Button > Save As | F12 |
| File > Page Setup | Page Layout > Page Setup (click dialog box launcher for more options) | *In Word 2003:* Alt-F, U |
| | *or* | *In Word 2007:* Alt-P, SP |
| | Office Button > Print > Print Preview > Page Setup (click dialog box launcher for more options) | |
| File > Print Preview | Office Button > Print > Print Preview | Alt-Ctrl-I |
| File > Print | Office Button > Print | Ctrl-P |
| File > Recently Used Documents | Office Button > Recent Documents | Alt-F |
| **"Edit" Menu:** | | |
| Edit > Undo | Quick Access toolbar > Undo icon | Ctrl-Z |
| Edit > Redo | Quick Access toolbar > Redo icon | Ctrl-Y |
| Edit > Cut | Home > Clipboard > Cut | Ctrl-X |
| Edit > Copy | Home > Clipboard > Copy | Ctrl-C |
| Edit > Office Clipboard | Home > Clipboard dialog box launcher | *In Word 2003:* Ctrl-C, Ctrl-C |
| | | *In Word 2007:* Alt-H, F, O |
| Edit > Paste | Home > Clipboard > Paste | Ctrl-V |

| Word 2003 Location | Word 2007 Location | Keyboard Shortcut |
|---|---|---|
| Edit > Paste Special | Home > Clipboard > Paste > Paste Special | *In Word 2003:* Alt-E, S |
| | | *In Word 2007:* Alt-E, S *or* Alt-Ctrl-V |
| Edit > Paste as Hyperlink | Home > Clipboard > Paste > Paste as Hyperlink | Alt-E, H |
| Edit > Select All | Home > Editing > Select > Select All | Ctrl-A |
| Edit > Find | Home > Editing > Find | Ctrl-F |
| Edit > Replace | Home > Editing > Replace | Ctrl-H |
| Edit > Go To | Home > Editing > Find > Go To | Ctrl-G |
| **"View" Menu:** | | |
| View > Normal | View > Document Views > Draft | Alt-Ctrl-N |
| View > Web Layout | View > Document Views > Web Layout | Alt-V, W |
| View > Print Layout | View > Document Views > Print Layout | Alt-Ctrl-P |
| View > Reading Layout | View > Document Views > Full Screen Reading | Alt-V, R |
| View > Outline | View > Document Views > Outline | Alt-Ctrl-O |
| View > Task Pane | The overall task pane is gone in Word 2007, but some dialog box launchers display task panes. | *In Word 2003:* Ctrl-F1 |
| | | *In Word 2007:* not available |
| View > Toolbars | Word 2007 no longer has toolbars. | *In Word 2003:* Alt-V, T |
| | | *In Word 2007:* not available |
| View > Ruler | View > Show/Hide > Ruler | Alt-V, L |
| | *or* | |
| | Office Button > Print > Print Preview > Preview > Show/Hide Ruler | |
| View > Thumbnails | View > Show/Hide > Thumbnails | Alt-V, B |
| View > Header and Footer | Insert > Header & Footer | Alt-V, H |
| View > Footnotes | References > Footnotes > Show Notes | Alt-V, F |
| View > Markup | Review > Tracking > Show Markup | Alt-V, A |
| View > Full Screen | View > Document Views > Full Screen Reading | Alt-V, U |
| View > Zoom | Status Bar > Zoom Slider | Alt-V, Z |
| | *Or View > Zoom* | |

| Word 2003<br>Location | Word 2007<br>Location | Keyboard<br>Shortcut |
|---|---|---|
| **"Insert" Menu:** | | |
| Insert > Break | Insert > Pages > Page Break | Alt-I, B |
| Insert > Page Numbers | Insert > Header & Footer > Page Number | Alt-I, U |
| | *or* | |
| | Header & Footer Tools > Design > Header & Footer > Page Number | |
| Insert > Date and Time | Insert > Text > Date & Time | Alt-I, T |
| | *or* | |
| | Header & Footer Tools > Design > Insert > Date & Time | |
| Insert > AutoText | Insert > Text > Quick Parts | *In Word 2003:* Alt-I, A |
| | | *In Word 2007:* Alt-N, Q |
| Insert > Field | Insert > Text > Quick Parts > Field | Alt-I, F |
| | *or* | |
| | Header & Footer Tools > Design > Insert > Quick Parts > Field | |
| Insert > Symbol | Insert > Symbols > Symbol | *In Word 2003:* Alt-I, S |
| | | *In Word 2007:* Alt-I, S *or* Alt-N, U |
| Insert > Comment | Review > Comments > New Comment | Alt-Ctrl-M |
| Insert > References | All Reference commands are now located under the References ribbon tab. | *In Word 2003:* Alt-I, N |
| | | *In Word 2007:* Alt-S |
| Insert > Picture | All Picture commands are located under Insert > Illustrations, with the following exceptions: | *In Word 2003:* Alt-I, P |
| | • WordArt is located in Insert > Text > WordArt | *In Word 2007:* Alt-N |
| | • From Scanner or Camera is not included in Word 2007 | |
| Insert > Text Box | Insert > Text > Text Box | *In Word 2003:* Alt-I, X |
| | | *In Word 2007:* Alt-N, X |
| Insert > File | Insert > Text > Object > Text from File | Alt-I, L |
| Insert > Object | Insert > Text > Object | Alt-I, O |
| Insert > Bookmark | Insert > Links > Bookmark | Alt-I, K |
| Insert > Hyperlink | Insert > Links > Hyperlink | Ctrl-K |

| Word 2003 Location | Word 2007 Location | Keyboard Shortcut |
|---|---|---|
| **"Format" Menu:** | | |
| Format > Font | Home > Font (click dialog box launcher for more options) | Ctrl-D |
| Format > Paragraph | Home > Paragraph (click dialog box launcher for more options) | Alt-O, P |
| | *or* | |
| | Page Layout > Paragraph (click dialog box launcher for more options) | |
| Format > Bullets and Numbering | Home > Paragraph > Bullets icon | *In Word 2003:* Alt-O, N |
| | *or* | *In Word 2007:* Alt-O, N *or* Alt-H, N/U |
| | Home > Paragraph > Numbering icon | |
| | *or* | |
| | Office Button > Word Options > Customize > All Commands > Bullets and Numbering | |
| Format > Borders and Shading | Home > Paragraph > Shading icon | *In Word 2003:* Alt-O, B |
| | *or* | *In Word 2007:* Alt-O, B *or* Alt-H, B/H |
| | Home > Paragraph > Arrow next to the most recently used command: a border command | |
| | *or* | |
| | Horizontal Line, Draw Table, View Gridlines, or Borders and Shading | |
| Format > Columns | Page Layout > Page Setup > Columns | *In Word 2003:* Alt-O, C |
| | | *In Word 2007:* Alt-O, C *or* Alt-P, J |
| Format > Tabs | Home > Paragraph dialog box launcher > Tabs | Alt-O, T |
| Format > Change Case | Home > Font > Change Case icon | *In Word 2003:* Alt-O, E |
| | | *In Word 2007:* Alt-O, E *or* Alt-H, 7 |
| Format > AutoFormat | Office Button > Word Options > Customize > All Commands > AutoFormat | Alt-Ctrl-K *or* Alt-O, A |
| Format > Styles and Formatting | Home > Styles | Alt-O, S |
| Format > Reveal Formatting | Office Button > Word Options > Customize > All Commands > Reveal Formatting | Alt-O, V |

| Word 2003<br>Location | Word 2007<br>Location | Keyboard<br>Shortcut |
|---|---|---|
| **"Tools" Menu:** | | |
| Tools > Spelling and Grammar | Review > Proofing > Spelling & Grammar | F7 |
| Tools > Research | Review > Proofing > Research | Alt-Click |
| Tools > Word Count | Status bar > Words | Ctrl-Shift-G |
| | *or* | |
| | Review > Proofing > Word Count | |
| Tools > AutoSummarize | Office Button > Word Options > Customize > All Commands > AutoSummary Tools | Alt-T, U |
| Tools > Track Changes | Review > Tracking > Track Changes | Ctrl-Shift-E |
| Tools > Compare and Merge Documents | Review > Compare > Compare | *In Word 2003:* Alt-T, D |
| | | *In Word 2007:* Alt-T, D *or* Alt-R, M, C |
| Tools > Letters and Mailings | Mailings | *In Word 2003:* Alt-T, E |
| | | *In Word 2007:* Alt-M |
| Tools > Macro | View > Macros > Macros | *In Word 2003:* Alt-T, M |
| | *or* | *In Word 2007:* Alt-W, M |
| | Developer > Code > Macros | |
| Tools > Templates and Add-Ins | Developer > Templates > Document Template | Alt-T, I |
| Tools > AutoCorrect Options | Office Button > Word Options > Proofing > AutoCorrect Options | Alt-T, A |
| Tools > Customize | Office Button > Word Options > Customize | *In Word 2003:* Alt-T, C |
| | | *In Word 2007:* Alt-F, I, C |
| Tools > Options | Office Button > Word Options | *In Word 2003:* Alt-T, O |
| | | *In Word 2007:* Alt-T, O *or* Alt-F, I |

| Word 2003 Location | Word 2007 Location | Keyboard Shortcut |
|---|---|---|
| **"Table" Menu:** | | |
| Table > Draw Table | Home > Paragraph > Borders icon > Draw Table | *In Word 2003:* Alt-A, W |
| | *or* | *In Word 2007:* Alt-A, W *or* Alt-N, T, D |
| | Insert > Tables > Table > Draw Table | |
| | *or* | |
| | Table Tools > Design > Draw Borders > Draw Table | |
| Table > Insert > Table | Insert > Tables > Table > Insert Table | *In Word 2003:* Alt-A, I, T |
| | | *In Word 2007:* Alt-A, I, T *or* Alt-N, T |
| Table > Insert > Columns, Rows, Cells | Table Tools > Layout > Rows & Columns | *In Word 2003:* Alt-A, I, choose addl. letter |
| | | *In Word 2007:* Alt-J, L, choose addl. letter |
| Table > Delete > Table, Columns, Rows, Cells | Table Tools > Layout > Rows & Columns > Delete | *In Word 2003:* Alt-A, D, choose addl. letter |
| | | *In Word 2007:* Alt-J, L, D, choose addl. letter |
| Table > Select > Table, Column, Row, Cell | Table Tools > Layout > Table > Select | *In Word 2003:* Alt-A, C, choose addl. letter |
| | | *In Word 2007:* Alt-J, L, K, choose addl. letter |
| Table > Merge Cells | Table Tools > Layout > Merge > Merge Cells | *In Word 2003:* Alt-A, M |
| | | *In Word 2007:* Alt-A, M *or* Alt-J, L, M |
| Table > Split Cells | Table Tools > Layout > Merge > Split Cells | *In Word 2003:* Alt-A, P |
| | | *In Word 2007:* Alt-A, P *or* Alt-J, L, P |
| Table > Split Table | Table Tools > Layout > Merge > Split Table | *In Word 2003:* Alt-A, T |
| | | *In Word 2007:* Alt-A, T *or* Alt-J, L, Q |
| Table > Table AutoFormat | Table Tools > Design > Table Styles | *In Word 2003:* Alt-A, F |
| | | *In Word 2007:* Alt-J, T, S |
| Table > AutoFit | Table Tools > Layout > Cell Size > AutoFit | *In Word 2003:* Alt-A, A |
| | | *In Word 2007:* Alt-J, L, F |

| Word 2003 Location | Word 2007 Location | Keyboard Shortcut |
|---|---|---|
| Table > Heading Rows Repeat | Table Tools > Layout > Data > Repeat Header Rows | *In Word 2003:* Alt-A, H |
| | | *In Word 2007:* Alt-A, H *or* Alt-J, L, J |
| Table > Convert > Text to Table | Insert > Tables > Table > Convert Text to Table | *In Word 2003:* Alt-A, V, X |
| | | *In Word 2007:* Alt-A, V, X *or* Alt-N, T, V |
| Table > Convert > Table to Text | Table Tools > Layout > Data > Convert to Text | *In Word 2003:* Alt-A, V, B |
| | | *In Word 2007:* Alt-A, V, B *or* Alt-J, L, V |
| Table > Sort | Home > Paragraph > Sort | *In Word 2003:* Alt-A, S |
| | *or* | *In Word 2007:* Alt-A, S *or* Alt-J, L, S, O |
| | Table Tools > Layout > Table > Sort | |
| Table > Formula | Table Tools > Layout > Table > Formula | *In Word 2003:* Alt-A, O |
| | | *In Word 2007:* Alt-A, O *or* Alt-J, L, U, L |
| Table > Hide/Show Gridlines | Table Tools > Layout > Table > Hide/Show Gridlines | *In Word 2003:* Alt-A, G |
| | | *In Word 2007:* Alt-A, G *or* Alt-J, L, T, G |
| Table > Table Properties | Table Tools > Layout > Table > Properties | *In Word 2003:* Alt-A, R |
| | *or* | *In Word 2007:* Alt-A, R *or* Alt-J, L, O |
| | Table Tools > Layout > Cell Size > Properties | |
| **"Window" Menu:** | | |
| Window > New Window | View > Window > New Window | Alt-W, N |
| Window > Arrange All | View > Window > Arrange All | Alt-W, A |
| Window > Compare Side by Side with | View > Window > View Side by Side | Alt-W, B |
| Window > Split/Remove Split | View > Window > Split/Remove Split | *Split:* Alt-Ctrl-S |
| | | *Remove Split:* Alt-Shift-C |
| Window > Currently Open Documents | View > Window > Switch Windows | *In Word 2003:* Alt-W |
| | | *In Word 2007:* Alt-W, W |

## *Appendix E*

## How To Change The Default Font Type And Size In MS Word

1) *Open a new document*

2) *Call up the Font dialog box: Format>Font*

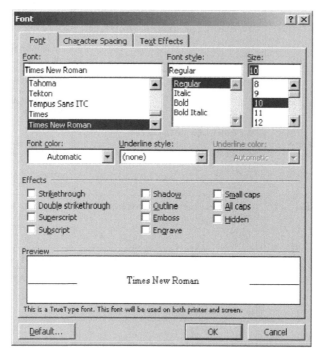

3) *Set your preferred font and click on the "Default" button (lower left of dialog box).*

Laurence Seton © | Projecteze Inc.

## *About The Author*

Laurence H. Seton is a Professional Engineer and a Project Management Professional (PMP) with the worldwide Project Management Institute. He has over 30 years of project management experience in manufacturing, land development, oil and gas, transportation, facility management, health care, training and management consulting.

Laurence's natural tendency is to be extremely well organized which has been an asset throughout his career. Since developing the Projecteze system, he has been able to maintain a healthy work-life balance and he uses Projecteze® to achieve success on all of his projects.

Equally rewarding for Laurence is having time to spend with his family and pursue many personal interests from playing hockey and learning guitar to scuba diving and researching his father's World War II experiences.

Laurence facilitates courses and consults to corporations on how they can fully benefit from integrating the Projecteze system into their business practice.

Laurence H. Seton lives in Calgary, Alberta, Canada.
He can be reached through the book website at
www.OnTopOfEverything.com.

CPSIA information can be obtained at www.ICGtesting.com
Printed in the USA
LVOW01s0529080514

384814LV00027BA/1807/P